Selected for reprinting by The Alaska Geographic Society as
Volume 7, Number 4, 1980 *ALASKA GEOGRAPHIC*®

Klondike Lost

A Decade of Photographs by Kinsey & Kinsey

Norm Bolotin

ALASKA NORTHWEST PUBLISHING COMPANY
ANCHORAGE, ALASKA

Editors: Robert A. Henning, Barbara Olds
Associate Editors: Margy Kotick, Penny Rennick
Designer: Jon.Hersh

Registered Trademark: *Alaska Geographic.*
ISSN 0361-1353; key title *Alaska Geographic.*
ISBN 0-88240-148-3

Library of Congress cataloging in publication data:
Bolotin, Norm, 1951-
Klondike lost.
(Alaska geographic; v. 7, no. 4 ISSN 0361-1353)
Includes photos. by Clarke and Clarence Kinsey.
Bibliography: p.
1. Grand Forks, Yukon — History. 2. Klondike gold fields. I. Kinsey, Clarke. II. Kinsey, Clarence. III. Title. IV. Series.
F901.A266 vol. 7, no.4 [F1095.5.G7] 917.98s
ISBN 0-88240-148-3 [971.9'1] 80-20533

ALASKA GEOGRAPHIC®, ISSN 0361-1353, is published quarterly by The Alaska Geographic Society, Anchorage, Alaska 99509. Second-class postage paid in Edmonds, Washington 98020. Printed in U.S.A.

THE ALASKA GEOGRAPHIC SOCIETY is a nonprofit organization exploring new frontiers of knowledge across the lands of the polar rim, learning how other men and other countries live in their Norths, putting the geography book back in the classroom, exploring new methods of teaching and learning—sharing in the excitement of discovery in man's wonderful new world north of 51°16'.

MEMBERS OF THE SOCIETY RECEIVE *Alaska Geographic®*, a quality magazine which devotes each quarterly issue to monographic in-depth coverage of a northern geographic region or resource-oriented subject.

MEMBERSHIP DUES in The Alaska Geographic Society are $20 per year; $24 to non-U.S. addresses. (Eighty percent of each year's dues is for a one-year subscription to *Alaska Geographic®*.) Order from The Alaska Geographic Society, Box 4-EEE, Anchorage, Alaska 99509; (907) 274-0521.

MATERIAL SOUGHT: The editors of *Alaska Geographic®* seek a wide variety of informative material on the lands north of 51°16' on geographic subjects—anything to do with resources and their uses (with heavy emphasis on quality color photography)—from Alaska, Northern Canada, Siberia, Japan—all geographic areas that have a relationship to Alaska in a physical or economic sense. In early 1980 editors were seeking material on the following geographic regions and subjects: the Kobuk-Noatak area, the Seward Peninsula and glaciers of Alaska.We do not want material done in excessive scientific terminology. A query to the editors is suggested. Payments are made for all material upon publication.

CHANGE OF ADDRESS: The post office does not automatically forward *Alaska Geographic®* when you move. To insure continuous service, notify us six weeks before moving. Send us your new address and zip code (and moving date), your old address and zip code, and if possible send a mailing label from a copy of *Alaska Geographic®*. Send this information to *Alaska Geographic®* Mailing Offices, 130 Second Avenue South, Edmonds, Washington 98020.

MAILING LISTS: We have begun making our members' names and addresses available to carefully screened publications and companies whose products and activities might be of interest to you. If you would prefer not to receive such mailings, please so advise us, and include your mailing label (or your name and address if label is not available).

About This Issue

KLONDIKE LOST: A Decade of Photographs by Kinsey & Kinsey has been selected for reprinting in its entirety as Volume 7, Number 4 of *ALASKA GEOGRAPHIC®* magazine.

Thousands of books and articles have been written about the Klondike gold rush, but no more than a few pages have ever been devoted to one of its greatest boom towns — the remarkable community of Grand Forks, once home to almost 10,000 people.

One of the finest photographic chronicles of the entire gold rush era was compiled by a pair of young Grand Forks photographers — Clarke and Clarence Kinsey. Clarke, like his older brother Darius, went on to national fame as a timber photographer for much of the first half of this century. But before that, he and Clarence recorded the life and death of Grand Forks, and with it, the Klondike gold rush era.

Norm Bolotin spent almost two years researching the town of Grand Forks — its miners, storekeepers, prostitutes and children; the hotels and the bars where they worked and played; the cabins where they lived and the churches where they prayed; and the gold mining that brought them all together. He utilized the Kinseys' photos; research facilities in Seattle, Juneau, Skagway, Whitehorse and Dawson City; and the recollections of the few people still living who had been in Grand Forks.

Bolotin has lived in Seattle all of his life, but has traveled extensively throughout Alaska and northwest Canada since 1973. In that time he has written hundreds of articles on the North for a variety of publications, including many which dealt with the people and events of Alaska and the Yukon Territory's colorful mining past. He joined the Alaska Northwest Publishing Company in 1978 as an *ALASKA®* magazine editor.

Any member of The Alaska Geographic Society who separately purchased a copy of the book edition of *KLONDIKE LOST* may return this volume and request that membership be extended by one issue. Requests should be addressed to The Alaska Geographic Society mailing offices, 130 Second Avenue South, Edmonds, Washington 98020.

The Kinseys' studio in Grand Forks, Yukon Territory. Built in 1902, this building was one of the most unique in Grand Forks. The huge skylight provided sunlight for studio work. The Commission House occupied the street level of the building. The lead horses are facing the main street of Grand Forks, the dirt road to the right where the stores and hotel were. In back of the studio was an apartment, where Clarence and Agnes and their daughter Olive later lived. Clarence Kinsey is standing at the door to the studio at the top of the stairs.

Alaska Geographic® Back Issues

The North Slope, Vol. 1, No. 1. Charter issue of *ALASKA GEOGRAPHIC®*. Out of print.

One Man's Wilderness, Vol. 1, No. 2. The story of a dream shared by many, fulfilled by few: a man goes into the bush, builds a cabin and shares his incredible wilderness experience. Color photos. 116 pages, $7.95

Admiralty . . . Island in Contention, Vol. 1, No. 3. An intimate and multifaceted view of Admiralty: its geological and historical past, its present-day geography, wildlife and sparse human population. Color photos. 78 pages, $5.00

Fisheries of the North Pacific: History, Species, Gear & Processes, Vol. 1, No. 4. Out of print.

The Alaska-Yukon Wild Flowers Guide, Vol. 2, No. 1. First Northland flower book with both large, color photos and detailed drawings of every species described. Features 160 species, common and scientific names and growing height. 112 pages, $10.95.

Richard Harrington's Yukon, Vol. 2, No. 2. A collection of 277 stunning color photos by Canadian photographer-writer Richard Harrington captures the Yukon in all its seasons and moods, from Watson Lake to Herschel Island. 103 pages, $7.95

Prince William Sound, Vol. 2, No. 3. Out of print.

Yakutat: The Turbulent Crescent, Vol. 2, No. 4. Out of print.

Glacier Bay: Old Ice, New Land, Vol. 3, No. 1. The expansive wilderness of Southeastern Alaska's Glacier Bay National Monument unfolds in crisp text and color photographs. Records the flora and fauna of the area, its natural history, with hike and cruise information, plus a large-scale color map. 132 pages, $9.95

The Land: Eye of the Storm, Vol. 3, No. 2. Out of print.

Richard Harrington's Antarctic, Vol. 3, No. 3. The Canadian photojournalist guides readers through remote and little understood regions of the Antarctic and Subantarctic. More than 200 color photos and a large fold-out map. 104 pages, $8.95

The Silver Years of the Alaska Canned Salmon Industry: An Album of Historical Photos, Vol. 3, No. 4. Temporarily out of print.

Alaska's Volcanoes: Northern Link in the Ring of Fire, Vol. 4, No. 1. Scientific overview supplemented with eyewitness accounts of Alaska's historic volcano eruptions. Includes color and black-and-white photos and a schematic description of the effects of plate movement upon volcanic activity. 88 pages, $7.95

The Brooks Range: Environmental Watershed, Vol. 4, No. 2. Temporarily out of print.

Kodiak: Island of Change, Vol. 4, No. 3. Although half the size of New Jersey, and once the administrative center of Russian Alaska, the 3,588-square-mile island of Kodiak remains well off the beaten path. Past, present and future—everything from Russian exploration to the present-day quest for oil. Maps, color photos. 96 pages, $7.95

Wilderness Proposals: Which Way for Alaska's Lands?, Vol. 4, No. 4. Out of print.

Cook Inlet Country, Vol. 5, No. 1. A visual tour of the region—its communities, big and small, and its countryside. Begins at the southern tip of the Kenai Peninsula, circles Turnagain Arm and Knik Arm for a close-up view of Anchorage, and visits the Matanuska and Susitna valleys and the wild, west side of the inlet. 144 pages; 230 color photos, separate map. $9.95

Southeast: Alaska's Panhandle, Vol. 5, No. 2. Most colorful edition to date, exploring Southeastern Alaska's maze of fjords and islands, mossy forests and glacier-draped mountains—from Dixon Entrance to Icy Bay, including all of the state's fabled Inside Passage. Along the way are profiles of every town, together with a look at the region's history, economy, people, attractions and future. Includes large fold-out map and seven area maps. 192 pages, $12.95.

Bristol Bay Basin, Vol. 5, No. 3. Explores the land and the people of the region known to many as the commercial salmon-fishing capital of Alaska. Illustrated with contemporary color and historic black-and-white photos. Includes a large fold-out map of the region. 96 pages, $9.95.

Alaska Whales and Whaling, Vol. 5, No. 4. The wonders of whales in Alaska—their life cycles, travels and travails—are examined, with an authoritative history of commercial and subsistence whaling in the North. Includes a fold-out poster of 14 major whale species in Alaska in perspective, color photos and illustrations, with historical photos and line drawings. 144 pages, $9.95.

Yukon-Kuskokwim Delta, Vol. 6, No. 1. Temporarily out of print.

The Aurora Borealis, Vol. 6, No. 2. The northern lights — in ancient times seen as a dreadful forecast of doom, in modern days an inspiration to countless poets. Here one of the world's leading experts — Dr. S.-I. Akasofu of the University of Alaska — explains in an easily understood manner, aided by many diagrams and spectacular color and black-and-white photos, what causes the aurora, how it works, how and why scientists are studying it today and its implications for our future. 96 pages, $7.95.

Alaska's Native People, Vol. 6, No. 3. In the largest edition to date—result of several years of research—the editors examine the varied worlds of the Inupiat Eskimo, Yup'ik Eskimo, Athabascan, Aleut, Tlingit, Haida and Tsimshian. Most photos are by Lael Morgan, *ALASKA®* magazine's roving editor, who since 1974 has been gathering impressions and images from virtually every Native village in Alaska. Included are sensitive, informative articles by Native writers, plus a large, four-color map detailing the Native villages and defining the language areas. 304 pages, $19.95.

The Stikine, Vol. 6, No 4. River route to three Canadian gold strikes in the 1800s, the Stikine is the largest and most navigable of several rivers that flow from northwestern Canada through Southeastern Alaska on their way to the sea. This edition explores 400 miles of Stikine wilderness, recounts the river's paddlewheel past and looks into the future, wondering if the Stikine will survive as one of the North's great free-flowing rivers. Illustrated with contemporary color photos and historic black-and-white; includes a large fold-out map. 96 pages, $9.95.

Alaska's Great Interior, Vol. 7, No. 1. Alaska's rich Interior country, west from the Alaska-Yukon Territory border and including the huge drainage between the Alaska Range and the Brooks Range, is covered thoroughly. Included are the region's people, communities, history, economy, wilderness areas and wildlife. Illustrated with contemporary color and black-and-white photos. Includes a large fold-out map. 128 pages, $9.95.

A Photographic Geography of Alaska, Vol. 7, No. 2. An overview of the entire state—a visual tour through the six regions of Alaska: Southeast, Southcentral/Gulf Coast, Alaska Peninsula and Aleutians, Bering Sea Coast, Arctic and Interior. Plus a handy appendix of valuable information—"Facts About Alaska." Approximately 160 color and black-and-white photos and 35 maps. 192 pages, $17.95.

The Aleutians, Vol. 7, No. 3. The fog-shrouded Aleutians are many things — home of the Aleut, a tremendous wildlife spectacle, a major World War II battleground and now the heart of a thriving new commercial fishing industry. Roving editor Lael Morgan contributes most of the text; also included are contemporary color and black-and-white photographs, and a large fold-out map. 224 pages, $14.95.

COMING ATTRACTION

Wrangell-Saint Elias, Vol. 8, No. 1. Mountains, including the continent's second- and fourth-highest peaks, dominate this international wilderness that sweeps from the Wrangell Mountains in Alaska to the southern Saint Elias range in Canada. The region draws backpackers, mountain climbers, and miners, and is home for a few hardy, year-round inhabitants. Illustrated with contemporary color and historical black-and-white photographs. Includes a large fold-out map. To be distributed to members in February 1981. Price to be announced.

Massive Mount Logan (19,850 feet) and pointed Mount Augusta (14,070 feet) dominate the skyline in this view of the Saint Elias Mountains. (George Herben)

Your $20 membership in The Alaska Geographic Society includes 4 subsequent issues of *ALASKA GEOGRAPHIC®*, the Society's official quarterly. Please add $4 for non-U.S. membership.

Additional membership information available upon request. Single copies of the *ALASKA GEOGRAPHIC®* back issues available, per listing here. When ordering please add $1 postage/handling per copy. To order back issues send your check or money order and volumes desired to:

The Alaska Geographic Society

Box 4-EEE, Anchorage, AK 99509

GOLD! When that word reached the outside world in July 1897, nearly a year after its discovery in Yukon's Rabbit Creek (later renamed Bonanza Creek) the rush to the Klondike began. Would-be prospectors crowded steamships; stampeders with gear-laden pack animals inched up snowy mountain passes in bitter cold; and tent towns, hastily thrown together, boomed into communities such as Dawson City, Whitehorse, and one about which little has been written, Grand Forks.

At the juncture of Eldorado and Bonanza creeks, on what has been considered the richest ground in history, the town of Grand Forks was second only to Dawson as the largest community in the North and one of the largest in western Canada.

KLONDIKE LOST is the story of Grand Forks and the people who lived there. History brought to life through the Gold Rush-era photographs of Clarke and Clarence Kinsey, who themselves were among the miners who lived along the creeks at Grand Forks, and through the research of author Norm Bolotin.

We are pleased to acquaint members of The Alaska Geographic Society with this fascinating, little-known segment of northern history with this reprint of KLONDIKE LOST: A Decade of Photographs by Kinsey & Kinsey.

Robert A. Henning

President
The Alaska Geographic Society

For my parents

Contents

During its peak years, 1900-1902, Grand Forks was the center of activity for more than 10,000 people. Holidays were always special occasions and Klondikers made the most of them by combining celebrations for Canada's Dominion Day (July 1) with the United States' Independence Day (July 4). There were parades, races and various competitions for the entire population.

Introduction

Since the publication of my own history of the Klondike gold rush more than twenty years ago, I have watched with growing enthusiasm the numerous additions to Klondike literature and lore that have appeared. Recently, in a store in Whitehorse, I counted more than fifty books dealing with the Yukon or some aspect of the great stampede.

Curiously, until now, there has been very little focus on Grand Forks, the boom town at the juncture of Eldorado and Bonanza creeks, where lay the richest ground in history. Grand Forks was second only to Dawson as the largest community in the North and, indeed, one of the largest in western Canada. Grand Forks deserves its own chroniclers and those chroniclers have now appeared in the form of Clarke and Clarence Kinsey and their Boswell, Norm Bolotin.

In many ways Grand Forks was a more interesting town than Dawson for it was here that the "kings" of Eldorado, the Stanleys and the Berrys, Big Alex McDonald, Antone Stander and many others, had their headquarters. And it was here that the incomparable Belinda Mulroney (or Mulrooney—we have been given both spellings) held sway.

In Seattle, in the mid-fifties, while doing research for my own book, I was told that Miss Mulroney, now Mrs. Charles Carbonneau, was still alive and thought to be living in the vicinity. I searched the phone book in vain but then, in a drugstore directory, discovered that a Mrs. C. Carbonneau lived on the very outskirts of the city.

I hired a taxi and drove out to a small cottage on a suburban street. I knocked on the door. A small, elderly lady opened it.

"Are you by any freak of chance, Belinda Mulroney?" I asked her.

She stuck out a hand.

"Come on in, m'friend," said she. "We got a lot to talk about."

And for the next several hours we talked about her own career in general and Grand Forks in particular.

The Countess de Carbonneau, as she sometimes dubbed herself, is long gone now; but I am happy to see that her personality lingers on in these pages.

Mr. Bolotin's book is a valuable, indeed an essential chapter in the history of the Yukon Territory and the great stampede. All of us who care about preserving that history welcome it.

Pierre Berton
Kleinburg, Ontario

Inside the Kinseys' studio building the shelves were cluttered with boxes of photographic supplies and a collection of prints. Several of these portraits are of family members. Second from right in the top row of photos is a portrait of Clarence, and two photos to the left of that one, is a picture of his brother Darius. The round photo below Clarence is of their mother, Louisa Kinsey.

Preface

The Kinsey name has, to a degree, been discovered only recently. Darius Kinsey and his younger brother Clarke were well-known in the American timber industry for nearly half of the 20th century; both were widely respected for their striking and accurate portrayal of West Coast logging and the people who lived and worked in the timber camps—for days, for summers and sometimes for lifetimes.

Seattle's Superior Publishing Company released a volume on logging many years ago, highlighting the industry, but never really showing the excellent quality of the craftsman it featured—Darius Kinsey. Author Dave Bohn and Chronicle Books of San Francisco recently added much to our knowledge of the Kinseys when he obtained thousands of Darius's glass plate negatives and researched the family history. Chronicle issued a book that showed just what an artisan Darius was. That book, *Kinsey Photographer,* is appropriately subtitled *A Half Century of Negatives by Darius and Tabitha May Kinsey.*

But Darius and his wife Tabitha did not have exclusive title to that half-century of Kinsey photographic excellence. Clarke's career paralleled that of Darius.

For the Kinsey youngsters growing up in Snoqualmie, Washington, there was indeed a portent of things to come when Darius and Clarke formed the first Kinsey & Kinsey partnership. They operated out of a tent studio and traveled throughout much of what is now the Greater Seattle area, photographing individuals, businesses and serving as official photographers for a local railroad, The Snoqualmie, Lakeshore and Eastern.

That Kinsey partnership was short-lived, however, as the older Darius left home and began a very long and successful career as a photographer, operating out of Woolley (now Sedro Woolley), Washington. Clarke pursued his part-time photography and then went north when gold was discovered in the Klondike. His new partner was Clarence Kinsey—again there was a team of brothers known as Kinsey & Kinsey.

Until recently, the Kinsey & Kinsey logo—rough block type at the bottom of old and faded prints—was familiar only to a few history enthusiasts who had seen miscellaneous prints in libraries, archives or tacked to decaying walls somewhere. These individuals and a few Kinsey family members thought little of the Kinseys' Klondike work for years. Mention of the Kinsey name usually brought one familiar reaction: "You mean the timber photographer." Few people outside the timber industry were even aware that there was more than one Kinsey recording logging from British Columbia to California.

The technical quality of that timber photography outshines the work Clarke and Clarence accomplished in the Klondike. From the turn of the century to the 1950's, a great many excellent photographers recorded the events of the day, including that of the timber industry. The Kinsey logging photographs are excellent, and stand above and apart from the work of others as a piece of history. But the few hundred remaining Kinsey Klondike images stand apart from others in history for a very different reason: They show a segment of history previously unrecorded, or more accurately, previously unpublished.

Numerous photographers went north with the discovery of gold, and because many were there and several were so talented, we have a remarkably accurate log of the great rush to the Klondike. And there exists an excellent record of life in Dawson and across Alaska in Nome, much of this the work of E.A. Hegg.

Most everyone taking photographs in those hectic and exciting Klondike days lived in Dawson; however, Clarke and Clarence lived near their gold claim, along the creeks at Grand Forks. Until now, the written history of that community amounted to a few isolated pages of text and the photographic log of the people and their lives there was virtually nonexistent.

Clarke and Clarence worked under less than ideal conditions, and many of their photographs—like much work done in that time and region—show the effects of guesswork chemistry, cold winters and often long waits for supplies from Outside. Some of the glass plate negatives became scratched or broken, not an uncommon occurrence. The Kinseys were commercial photographers, but they went north to live the gold era, not just to photograph it. Because of this, their work offers an excellent diary of life among the several thousand miners, laborers, merchants, wives and children who called Grand Forks home.

When Clarke and Clarence left the Klondike, long after most of the others had, they left behind hundreds—probably thousands—of glass plate negatives that were too bulky to carry back to Snoqualmie. The plates they kept were the ones that were important to them—those of their friends and their family, their parties and their homes, their mines and their hard work.

After finding this collection of Kinsey photographs, I realized they told a remarkably different story of the gold rush era and the years that followed. But this story was somewhat like the first half of a two-part serial, incomplete without the names, anecdotes, tragedies and facts. After two years of research I have been fortunate to discover the town of Grand Forks and the people who lived there—an important part of gold rush history few ever realized even existed.

Norm Bolotin
Seattle, Washington

Louisa Kinsey (top) and Clarence (left) and Clarke Kinsey.

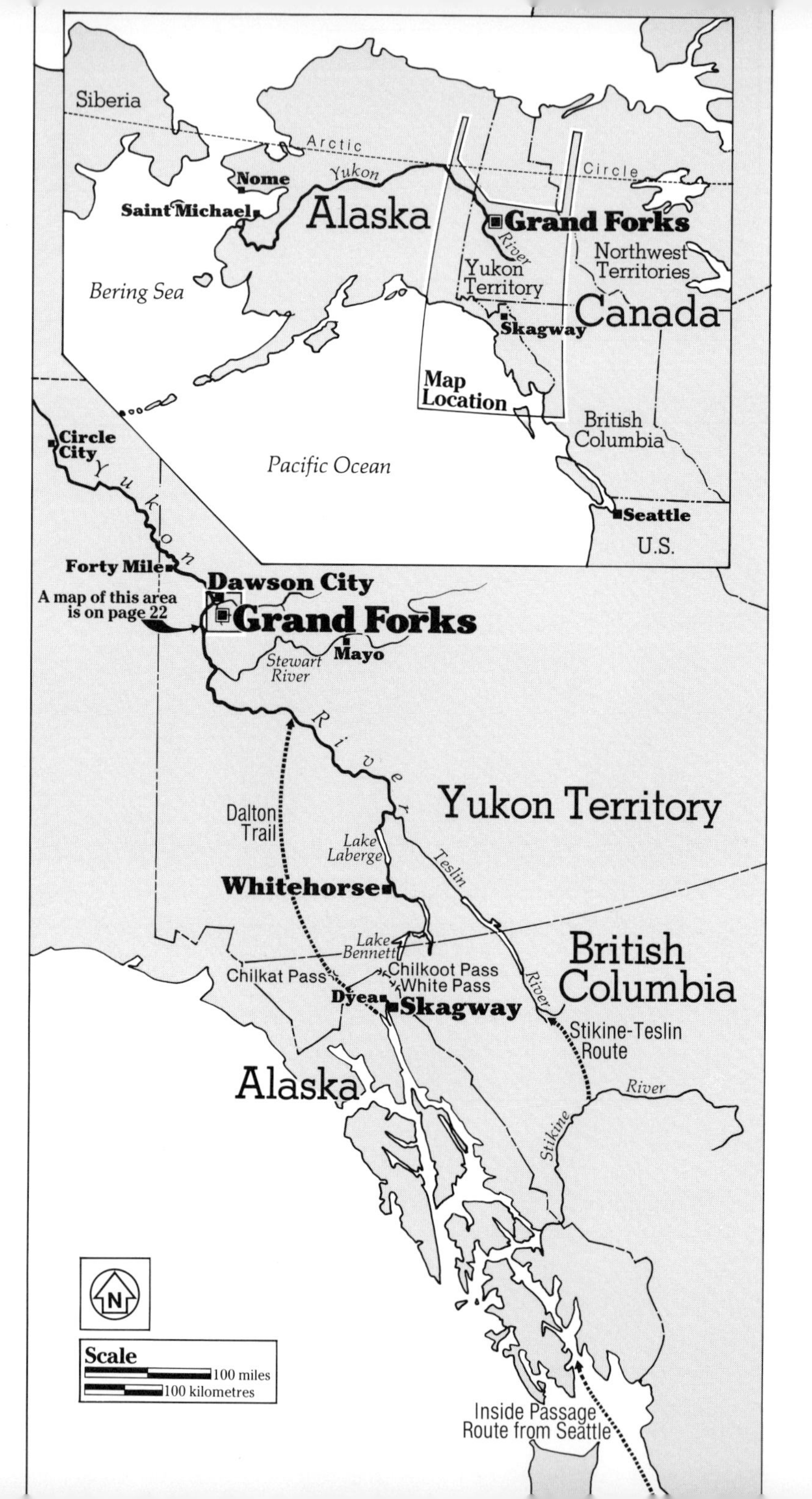

—I—

Klondike Beginnings

The discovery of gold that led to the rush was made in August 1896, nearly a year before the first Klondike gold found its way Outside and started the human stampede.

Robert Henderson, who had spent years looking for gold, is generally credited with the Klondike discovery. He is the one reputed to have pointed George Washington Carmack in the right direction. Carmack, who had a reputation for being lazy at best, promised to tell Henderson if he found gold. Carmack and his Indian brothers-in-law were on a fishing excursion when they found gold in Rabbit Creek, about fourteen miles from Dawson City. By the time Henderson heard the news, hundreds of other miners from throughout the North were already heading toward the Klondike and he was far behind. Rabbit Creek was quickly renamed Bonanza, and most of the miners who staked the claims along Bonanza, and along other creeks destined to become famous, were already in the Yukon or Alaska when gold was discovered. Most of the richest finds were made in 1896 and early 1897, before the rest of the world even knew gold had been discovered. Still, whether they were early or late, the people came, and a few of them got lucky; but in any case they all shared an incredible adventure. It was July 1897, eleven months after the first gold discovery was made, when the outside world heard the news. That was when Seattleite Tom

In the early days in the Klondike, the miners built bonfires to thaw the frozen ground, then dug the gold-bearing gravel out and shoveled it into long wooden boxes called sluices. Stream water was channeled through the sluices to wash out the dirt and rock, leaving the gold in the slats, or riffles, at the bottom of the boxes.

Lippy stepped off the steamer *Excelsior* in San Francisco with a suitcase weighted down with $50,000 in gold dust from his rich Klondike claim. By the time the second gold ship, the *Portland*, arrived in Seattle two days later, the rush was on.

From roughly 1897 until just before the end of the century, people from virtually every corner of the world and from every conceivable background headed toward the Klondike. Some were wealthy when they arrived, penniless when they left. A very few were just the opposite. Either way, the odds were stacked incredibly high against everyone who tried to reach the Klondike.

Only about half of all who started for the gold fields ever reached them. And only about half of those even got as far as staking a claim. The others worked the mines, operated businesses or found work in stores, saloons and stables. Of those who did mine, many found at least some gold. But perhaps no more than a hundred "struck it rich," a vague term that meant anything from finding a hundred thousand dollars to a few million.

Prior to this period, Edmund and Louisa Kinsey found the lure of western America too much to resist. They and their six children left Maryville, West Virginia, in 1890 for a new, and they hoped, exciting life in the Pacific Northwest.

The Kinseys settled about thirty miles east of Seattle in the small community of Snoqualmie, where they purchased the town's first commercial lot and built the town's first hotel. Louisa missed becoming the first woman in Snoqualmie by just a few days. It was an exciting time for the family and as much of an adventure as a new life for the children, most of whom were grown. Alfred, the oldest, was 22; Darius, 20; Clarence, 18; Emeline, 17; Edmund, 14; and the youngest, Clarke (who later added the *e* to the end of his name), 13.

There, in the family's new hotel, Clarke, Clarence and Darius were enthralled with a guest, remembered now only as Mr. Reynolds or Mr. Reinhardt; he stayed about a year, providing the three youngsters with an informal but complete education in the use of the large view cameras of the day.

When Clarke was 18 and Darius 25, they formed a photography partnership that lasted from 1895 to 1898. The two young men traveled to the small communities in the area, setting up temporary tent studios and doing portrait work. They also worked briefly with a friend from Blaine, Washington, named Bullock, advertising themselves in 1895 as Kinsey & Bullock, Photographers. However, the business was mostly a twosome—Kinsey & Kinsey.

Clarke and Darius also began their long careers in industrial photography at this time, serving as photographers for a local railroad, the Snoqualmie, Lakeshore and Eastern Railway. Then Darius decided to open his own studio in the town of Woolley (now Sedro Woolley) about forty-five miles north of Snoqualmie.

It was 1898. The area was alive with the news of the Klondike gold discovery. Clarence, 26, and Clarke, a newlywed and just 21, formed a new Kinsey & Kinsey partnership and with Clarke's wife Mary booked passage out of Seattle on a steamer for Skagway.

The Trip North

The Kinseys took the same route north as the majority of those who headed toward the Klondike from Seattle, San Francisco, Portland or Victoria. The route was by steamer up the sheltered waters of the Inside Passage, past Juneau and north on Lynn Canal to Skagway and Dyea. About ten percent continued on to the Bering Sea coast and to Saint Michael, at the mouth of the Yukon River, across Norton Sound from present-day Nome. At Saint Michael they boarded flat-bottomed riverboats for the 1,600-mile journey to Dawson, boom town of the Klondike.

Most of those who headed for the Klondike went via Chilkoot Pass. The pass, the most well-known element of the rush, led out of Dyea, a once tiny settlement that suddenly had a population of several thousand. (White Pass, just outside of Skagway, was not as steep, but it was much more rugged.) Aerial tramways, some several miles long, led over the Chilkoot from Dyea by the time the Kinseys made the trek in the second year of the rush. It was these tramways that kept Dyea in competition with Skagway with its large wharf.

It was not enough for a would-be miner to reach the top of a pass, however; once at the border of Canada, he (or she) was greeted by the North West Mounted Police who required anyone entering the country to possess a year's worth of supplies—or roughly 1,500 pounds in necessities. Those without the supplies were turned back. There is no way of knowing how many lives the Canadians saved with their unpopular insistence that miners be equipped for the conditions ahead.

An important—and difficult—part of the trip north was the overland and water route from the passes into the Klondike. One stop along the way was Lake Laberge, where the would-be miners had to stop to cut timber and build scows.

ALASKA OUTFITTERS   AMERICAN OUTFITTERS

T. M. DAULTON, President. C. P. BLANCHARD, Manager.

THE SEATTLE CLOTHING CO.

716 Second Avenue, Hinckley Block, SEATTLE, WASH.

SEATTLE, WASHINGTON, is acknowledged to be the **SHORTEST, CHEAPEST and BEST ROUTE** to the **Alaska Gold Fields** and the large majority will come and outfit here.

It will be well to bear in mind that many articles are produced and manufactured locally and are sold more reasonably than in Eastern cities.

Don't Waste Your Money buying useless articles in the East and paying freight charges across the continent to find on arrival at Seattle that you might have saved from 25 to 50 percent, besides purchasing a better and more complete outfit here.

We are receiving letters from all parts of the United States making inquiries about the cost of Provisions and Hardware, and have given below "Supplies for One Man for One Year," with prices prevailing at the present time. These prices, however, are subject to fluctuation.

The cost of this outfit depends upon the wants and tastes of the purchaser. Our advice is: "There is no economy in trying to save a few dollars on the purchase price of an outfit in the transportation of which is expended unceasing toil and hardships, and upon which your life depends." Buy the **best**. It goes farther and is more satisfactory.

Everything sold by us is put up by Experienced Packers in such a manner that it will reach its destination in perfect order.

SUPPLIES FOR ONE MAN FOR ONE YEAR.

CLOTHING.

Suit Corduroy	$ 12.50
Suit Oil Clothing	2.25 to 3.25
Mackinaw Coat	3.50 to 6.00
Suits Underwear	2.00 to 8.00
Sweaters	1.00 to 10.00
Caps	.25 to 5.00
Pairs Socks	.25 to 1.25
Pairs Mits	.15 to 2.50
Heavy Overshirts	1.50 to 5.00
Knit Scarf	.50 to 1.50
Pairs Overalls	.50 to 2.50
Jumpers	.50 to 1.50
Sleeping Bag	10.00 to 20.00
Fur Coats	6.00 to 50.00
Pairs German Socks	.75 to 1.25
Pairs Heavy Blankets	5.00 to 20.00
Pairs Mackinaw Pants	3.50 to 5.50
Suit of Blanket-Lined Duck	3.25 to 7.50
Chamois Underwear	
Buckskin Suits	
Fur Robes	

FOOTWEAR.

Pairs Rubber Boots	$ 4.00 to 6.50
Pairs Overs for German Socks	2.00 to 3.00
Pairs Overs for Felt Boots	.75 to 1.15
Pairs Miners' and Prospectors' Shoes	2.75 to 5.50
Pairs Arctic Socks	.25
Moccasins	2.00 to 3.00
Sole and Lace Leather; Rubber Cement and Patching; Thread, Wax, Needles, Awls; Shoe Nails; Repairing Outfits	1.00 to 2.50

MISCELLANEOUS.

Oil or Rubber Blankets	$ 1.25 to 3.50
Tent	4.50 up
Sled	5.00 up
Boat	18.00 to 30.00
Packs	1.00 up

One Price. Plain Figures.

PROVISIONS.

300 lbs.	Crown Flour, $5.00 bbl	$ 7.50
150 "	B. Bacon, 12½¢ lb.	18.75
25 "	Dry Salt Pork, 7¢ lb.	1.75
150 "	Bayo Beans, 3¢ lb.	4.50
25 "	Rolled Oats, 3¢ lb.	.75
25 "	Corn Meal, 1¼¢ lb.	.44
50 "	Rice, 6¢ lb.	3.00
100 "	Granulated Sugar, 6¢ lb.	6.00
25 "	Evaporated Potatoes, 15¢ lb.	3.75
10 "	Evaporated Onions, 35¢ lb.	3.50
25 "	Evaporated Apples, 8¢ lb.	2.00
10 "	Evaporated Apricots, 7¢ lb.	.70
15 "	Evaporated Peaches, 7¢ lb.	1.05
25 "	Evaporated Prunes, 8¢ lb.	2.00
10 "	Seedless Raisins, 8¢ lb.	.80
9 "	Soup Vegetables, 3 tins, 35¢ lb.	3.15
2 "	6 pots Ext. Beef, 4 oz., $1.25 lb.	2.50
1 lb.	Soup Tablets	.25
25 "	Eagle Cond. Milk, 2 doz. cans $2.	4.00
25 "	Ground Coffee, 5 lb. tins, 20¢ lb.	5.00
10 "	Tea, 1 lb. tins, 25¢ lb.	2.50
25 "	Smoked Beef, 20¢ lb.	5.00
8 "	Royal Baking Powder, 45¢ lb.	3.60
2 "	Yeast Cakes, 6 packages	.20

PROVISIONS—Continued.

4 "	Baking Soda, 7¢ lb.	.28
5 "	Dora Soap, 6 bars, 4¢ bar	.24
5 "	Tar Soap, 6 cakes, 8¢ cake	.48
30 "	Salt, 3 sacks, 8¢ sack	.24
1 lb.	Pepper	.30
1 "	Mustard, 4 tins, Coleman's, 15¢	.60
1 "	Ginger, 4 tins, 6¢ tin	.24
30 "	Hardtack, 5 tins, 5¢ lb.	1.50
50 "	Candles, 2 boxes, 240, $1.60 box	3.20
10 "	Matches, 1 gross	.35
5 "	Condensed Vinegar, 1 quart	1.00
2 "	Lime Juice, 1 quart	.50

HARDWARE.

Supplies for Two Men.

1 "Gold Nugget" Yukon Stove.
1 4-quart Granite-Covered Bucket.
1 6-quart Granite-Covered Bucket.
1 8-quart Granite-Covered Bucket.
1 No. 4 Steel Fry Pan.
1 3-quart Solid Lipped Coffee Pot.
2 9-inch Granite Plates.
2 Granite Cups.
2 Iron-handled Knives and Forks.
2 each, Tea and Table Spoons, tin.
2 Hunting Knives, in sheaths.
1 Heavy Forged Basting Spoon.
2 Hunter's Hatchets, in sheaths.
1 S. B. Handled Ax.
1 Pit Saw, complete.
1 Hand Saw.

HARDWARE—Continued.

1 Brace, 10-inch sweep.
1 Expansion Bit, boring from ½ to 1½ inches.
1 ¼-inch Auger Bit.
1 ⅝-inch Auger Bit.
1 Screw Driver Bit.
1 ¼-inch Socket Firmer Chisel.
1 Jack Plane, 1 Draw Knife, 1 Hammer.
2 8-inch Mill Files.
4 5-inch Slim Taper Files.
10 lbs. Assorted Nails.
5 balls Candle Wicking.
200 feet ½-inch Manila Rope.
2 Yukon Picks.
2 Half-spring Shovels.
2 Gold Pans.
1 6-inch Magnet.
2 Pairs Snow Glasses.
1 Gold Scale.
1 Pocket Compass.
1 Magnifying Glass.

Total cost for two men	$38.00
If for three men	41.00
If for four men	51.50

Additional Supplies for Two Men.

1 Tent, 10x12, 3-foot wall, 2 Hickory Yukon Sleighs, 1 Calking Iron, 5 lbs. Oakum, 8 lbs. Pitch, 2 pairs Snow Shoes.

Total cost	$31.00
If for three men	42.50
If for four men	51.00

All the above supplies to be of the best obtainable quality.

THE LARGEST ALASKA OUTFITTERS ON THE PACIFIC COAST.

All routes to the Klondike followed the Yukon River; it was the highway to Dawson and the gold fields. The Gov. Pingree, *shown here at Steamboat Slough, also operated as the* Bonanza King, *and was owned at various times by the Yukon Flyer Transportation Company and by the Boston & Alaska Transportation Company. The latter had visions of building an entire new town to rival Saint Michael, but failed to establish a successful loading point at the mouth of the Yukon.*

H. W. HARDY & Co.
DRUGS, STATIONERY AND CIGARS.

MILL HAVEN LUMBER Co.
ALL KINDS OF
LUMBER FOR SALE.
POST-OFFICE
HARDWARE.
STOVES, PAINTS, OILS, ROPE, PITCH.
Fred MacLennan.
HARDWARE.

Whitehorse, 320 miles from Dawson, was the only sizable settlement along the route from Skagway or Dyea into the Klondike. The town's permanence was assured with the completion of the White Pass & Yukon Route railway in 1900. The White Horse Hotel, to the right of the Grand, was managed by James Russell, who later ran the Vendome in Grand Forks. The hotel was advertised as "first class in every respect," and it offered weekly and monthly lodging as well as overnight accommodations for those on their way into or out of the Klondike. The electrically lighted hotel also sold wine, liquor and cigars, and even had a restaurant.

To get from the passes to the Yukon, miners had to build or buy boats, and there were often traffic jams of people and wooden scows. During the Kinseys' stay in the North, Clarence spent at least some time piloting boats on Lake Laberge. This scene was photographed at the junction of the Thirtymile and Hootalinqua rivers.

In addition to the passes and the Yukon River via Saint Michael, there were other routes to the Klondike: the Stikine River (via Teslin) and the Dalton Trail (roughly paralleling the present Haines Highway over the Chilkat Pass). But they were longer and less direct, so few would-be miners used them. These routes did, however, provide an easier means of moving freight and livestock during the years that followed.

The overland portion of the trip to the Klondike was actually very short via either the Chilkoot Pass or White Pass. Lake Bennett was less than 50 miles from either. From the lake, it was 500 miles by water to Dawson. Boats were built on the shores of Lake Bennett, then sailed over the water or, in winter, over the ice.

The boat trip was rough, long and tiresome, but it was the passes that everyone remembered as the most rigorous part of the journey. Most of those who turned back made the decision to quit along the slow, difficult trails through White and Chilkoot passes.

Within a year after the Kinseys made the trip (by the summer of 1899), a would-be miner could have crossed one of the passes—White Pass—with relative ease; the White Pass & Yukon Route, then the continent's northernmost railway, had been pushed through the mountains from Skagway to Lake Bennett. But by then the rush was nearly over and the gold-bearing streams of the Klondike had been staked from end to end.

It was not long, in fact, until the passes and the towns leading to them were almost the same as they had been before gold was discovered. The train ended the need for the tramways and Dyea, and nearly overnight the town shrank back to a quiet, insignificant community of just a few people; within a few years it disappeared completely.

By July 1900 the railway was completed all the way to Whitehorse, Yukon Territory. The struggle through the passes was over, and Skagway, too, became a quiet little town.

Chilkoot Pass was silent and empty; White Pass was noisy and alive with the clatter of narrow-gauge steam engines. But both passes were littered with reminders of that incredible rush—tons of abandoned supplies, thousands of decaying animal carcasses and dozens of marked and unmarked human graves.

Many small boats made the river trip to Dawson, usually in an attempt to save time, but once past Lake Bennett, it was far safer to complete the journey on a Yukon steamer.

Dawson was the capital of the Klondike and the town Joe Ladue and his partners built on a $1,000 land investment. In its heyday, Dawson was home to as many as 25,000 and was the largest town west of Winnipeg, Manitoba, or north of Victoria, British Columbia. The Canadian government sent surveyor William Ogilvie to assist Ladue in laying out the town. Ogilvie reported to his supervisors that Ladue "had laid out and disposed of a few lots for building, making his streets only 50 feet, and the main streets along the river even less, the builders going often close to the bank for convenience of getting water; but I stopped all that, and have the river front at least 66 feet wide, in most places more. All streets parallel to the rivers are 66 feet, and all at right angles to those I have left 50 feet, as Ladue had them. It seems to me that 50 feet is wide enough in this country, as it is hardly likely there will be much traffic on them."

The Early Years

Joseph Ladue, who had been in the North sixteen years when gold was discovered, went to Dawson before it was even so much as a tent town thrown together along the banks of the Yukon River. Ladue began obtaining as much land there as possible, applying to the Canadian government for patent to roughly 200 acres.

Ladue and his partners, Thomas Kirkpatrick and Arthur Harper, paid the $10-per-acre title conveyances and were given title to 100 acres; they formed the Dawson Townsite Company and Ladue also opened a lumbermill. It was 1897, just before the word of the previous year's gold discovery reached the Outside.

Ladue began selling the newly acquired land for $5 per building lot, turning Dawson into his personal gold mine and parlaying his real estate fortune into successful investments in gold mining properties, a steamship line and an expanded lumbermill.

When the Kinseys arrived in 1898, the town was bursting at the seams. The price of downtown lots had soared to $8,000; by 1899 some cost as much as $30,000. The Kinseys looked around and decided to move nearer the streams, where they could file their own claim and where they could photograph the miners at work.

And what they saw was not isolated miner-and-pan work along a stream where the gold was extracted simply by sifting loose gravel from shallow streambeds. To mine the Klon-

A rocker box, such as this one, was one way to clean up fines (very small particles of gold) or to keep working in winter, but it was slow. The gold was sifted through the box by rocking it like a cradle with the handle on the side.

dike, miners often had to dig for months before even reaching the gold-bearing gravel deep in the ground adjacent to the streams.

The early methods consisted of building fires to thaw the frozen ground. Miners would thaw and dig, thaw and dig until they had progressed through the frozen grass, dirt and muck. The typical gold vein, if there were such a thing, lay anywhere from 20 to 120 feet below the surface. There, in a gravel layer just above bedrock, was the gold-bearing paystreak—if one existed along that claim.

The depth and characteristics of the gold streaks varied from stream to stream and from hillside to hillside. But the gold was usually extracted from the bottom of that thawed column of earth, a shaft that had been shored up as the miners worked their way down. The shafts were as wide as possible, and as narrow as would suffice—depending on the time available and the patience of the crew.

Gravel from the bottom of the shaft was hauled up in buckets, and then the streams came into play. The diggings were shoveled into sluices—long wooden boxes—and the stream water was channeled through the sluices to wash out the dirt and rock, leaving the gold in the slats, or riffles, at the bottom of the boxes.

Later, Klondike mining became more sophisticated, but in the first years of the rush, it was pick, shovel and sluices—and hard work.

The size of the claims these miners worked made the mining anything but elbow to elbow, at least until most of the streams were staked and miners began hiring crews to work for them.

Canadian law granted the discoverer of a gold-bearing stream 1,000 feet of stream as his claim. Actually, all claims were 500 feet long, but the first locator was awarded rights to the discovery claim, plus a second immediately above or below, or a "double claim." Numbering then proceeded in both directions, with 500-foot-long claims numbered consecutively from the discovery claim. From then on a claim would be known by its number and when appropriate, with *above* or *below* added. On creek claims a miner was awarded rights to both sides of the stream back to the rimrock, up to a maximum total width of 2,000 feet. Hillside, or bench, claims extended from the stream claims back, and were 100 feet square. It was a bench claim that the Kinseys worked. While most miners tended to work stream claims first, many benches contained rich deposits of gold, but they were more difficult to work in the early years of Klondike mining because of the lack of water nearby.

Miners had to work their claims in winter or at least occupy them because they forfeited ownership if the mine sat idle. One way to guarantee that the mine was worked year-round was to give someone a "lay" on it—to let someone work it for a percentage of the cleanup the next spring. The disadvantage to giving a miner a lay was that he often would work the best land, leaving the harder work and lower-yield section of the claim for the owner. Many mine owners worked all winter and sluiced as late in the year as the streams flowed. By the last years of the 19th century, steam pumps were used so sluicing could continue into the fall and winter.

Belinda Mulrooney

In the early Klondike years there was only one other gold rush town besides Dawson. Known as both Grand Forks and Bonanza, it began as a small community a little more than fourteen miles from Dawson. It was referred to most frequently simply as the Forks because it was at the junction of Bonanza and Eldorado creeks. Dawson was the supply point and the city of businessmen like Ladue, of new miners unsure of where to go next and of dance hall girls and prostitutes eager to help them decide. Grand Forks was the quieter community where miners lived to be near their claims and where others lived to serve them.

A young, energetic woman named Belinda Mulrooney was responsible for the existence of this second town in the Klondike. She was the daughter of an Irish coal miner and had been raised in Scranton, Pennsylvania, a place she disliked immensely.

As a small child she had lived with her grandmother in Ireland and she longed to live again in an open, clean atmosphere.

Belinda was 20 when she packed her bags and went to the World Columbian Exposition in Chicago in 1892. Using her life's savings to buy a small piece of land, she opened a sandwich bar at the fair. The following year she sold out for $8,000 and moved to San Francisco, where she rented a small building and opened an ice cream parlor. She eventually lost her entire investment when the owners burned the building in a scheme to collect insurance money.

Belinda was angry, but she was not one to consider giving up. Instead, she signed on as a stewardess on the Pacific Coast Steamship Company's *City of Topeka,* a steamer which sailed to Skagway. Her voyages on the *Topeka* were like all of her efforts: marked by success most of the time, conducted with self-confidence all of the time.

On one occasion, when there was no doctor or experienced midwife on board, Belinda calmly delivered a baby while the captain stood on the other side of the cabin door and read instructions from a medical journal to her.

On another trip, a male passenger left a pair of dirty boots outside Belinda's cabin with instructions for her to polish them. She left the boots there with a note of her own, stating that if his boots showed up near her cabin again they would be returned—unpolished and full of sea water.

Belinda supplemented her income by trading hats and satin dresses to the Indian women in the villages along the coast. In exchange for the dresses and hats she received furs, which she sold to passengers for a profit. It is uncertain just how far her dealings went; perhaps they included various illegal and bootleg items, resulting in her having to pay the captain and purser a "commission" to allow her business ventures to continue.

Belinda heard of the Klondike gold discovery on one of her trips north, before the news reached the rest of the country. Gathering the items from her various dealings, she purchased more and headed for Dawson. She had $5,000

Belinda Mulrooney sold dresses and hats to Indian women when she worked as a stewardess on The City of Topeka. *She was paid in furs, which she sold at a handsome profit to passengers on the ship. Later, she traded in furs in the Klondike, too. "Sable and mink," she said later, "but the sable was really northern marten."*

worth of silk, cotton goods and hot water bottles with her when she stepped off the boat in Skagway and headed for the Chilkoot Pass.

Belinda was proud, but neither vain nor stupid. She signed on with a group of men at Lake Bennett, agreeing to wash and cook for them if they would take her and her supplies to Dawson. When she arrived, Belinda took her last half-dollar and tossed it into the Yukon. "I vowed I'd never need small change again," she said later. Belinda sold her $5,000 cache of supplies for $30,000 and began making plans to open a restaurant on Dawson's Front Street, which was the main street and ran along the Yukon River.

The real rush had not yet begun, but swarms of northern miners were already pouring into Dawson. Belinda decided there were too many businesses and not enough supplies in the growing city. She gave up her plans for a restaurant and moved closer to the streams and her potential customers. Many Dawson businessmen scoffed at her decision. They couldn't see the logic in anyone—especially a woman—going fourteen miles out of town to operate a business.

Many Klondike accounts credit Belinda with running a roadhouse, and numerous books written soon after the gold rush feature a photograph of a small log building called the Magnet, but it is very doubtful that this was ever hers. After her brief stop in Dawson, Belinda went immediately to Eldorado and Bonanza creeks in late 1897 and began hiring unemployed miners to build cabins and to start work on a two-story hotel; she was preparing for the onslaught of gold seekers she expected the next spring and summer. The Magnet Roadhouse was on Claim Number 17 Below Discovery on Bonanza, at least a mile from the site of Belinda's new hotel. A Mrs. M.P. Rothweiler ran it, and she too was self-assured and independent. Mrs. Rothweiler, who renamed the roadhouse Mary's Place, did not arrive and purchase the hostelry from its previous owner until 1898, at which time Belinda and the town of Grand Forks were already thriving.

Belinda had her crews go from claim to claim buying up any small boats that were available. She planned to resell some the next spring when there was a demand, and also to dismantle them and use the lumber for building—a typical practice in the area due to the scarcity of even rough-hewn lumber.

Belinda was a husky, strong woman, neat and tidy, with an air of self-assurance and knowledge. She never spoke a lot, but when she did speak she used only a few words to make it very clear what she meant. She learned quickly that the Klondike was a man's world, and the way to succeed in it was to know what she wanted—and to make sure others knew it as well.

Belinda's real interest, however, was in building a hotel. "I wasn't thinking of the money I'd make," she later said of her plans. She knew there would be a need for lodging the following spring and said she didn't want to see people freezing because they had nowhere to sleep. But she was also well aware of the profits she would make. Belinda supervised the construction of her 40- by 70-foot hotel, which was built from logs and chinked with grass, mud and moss; burlap, when available, also was used to insulate the outer walls of Klondike buildings. The new hotel was as nice as anything in Dawson and was just about the only thing

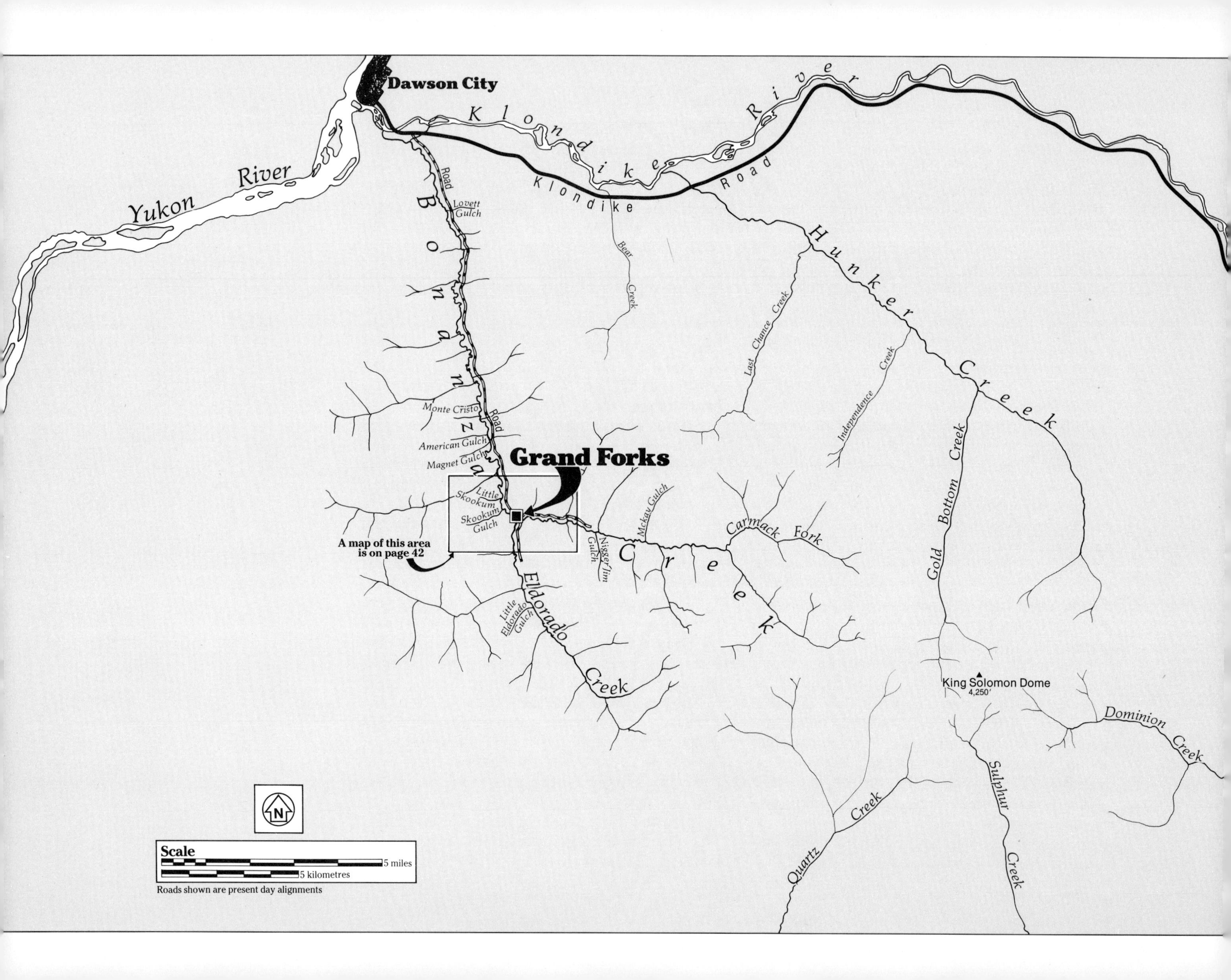

Dawson City
Yukon River
Klondike River
Klondike Road
Bonanza Road
Road
Lovett Gulch
Bear Creek
Hunker Creek
Last Chance Creek
Independence Creek
Monte Cristo
American Gulch
Magnet Gulch
Grand Forks
Little Skookum
Skookum Gulch
A map of this area is on page 42
Mckay Gulch
Nigger Jim Gulch
Carmack Fork
Bonanza Creek
Eldorado Creek
Little Eldorado Gulch
Gold Bottom Creek
King Solomon Dome
4,250′
Dominion Creek
Sulphur Creek
Quartz Creek
N
Scale
5 miles
5 kilometres
Roads shown are present day alignments

available outside of the town. Belinda even had a kennel built in back of the hotel, so her customers could keep their sled dogs nearby and comfortable.

Belinda named the new hotel for the forks of Eldorado and Bonanza where it was built, and, just as she expected, a town began growing around it. The town took its name from the hotel, and this was the Grand Forks that Clarke, Mary and Clarence Kinsey found when they arrived in 1898.

Belinda worked behind her bar at the Grand Forks Hotel, and she served the highest-priced liquor in the Klondike. But while her liquor was expensive, her meals, reputed to be twice as good as those offered in Dawson, sold for only about half the Dawson price. She even made sure that there was always a large bowl of homemade applesauce on each table in her dining room. The applesauce was made from dried apples, but it was the closest thing to fresh fruit most miners had seen in a long time and it was helpful in the continuing Klondike battle against scurvy.

Belinda always listened when she was serving drinks, letting her customers do most of the talking. She was attentive, smiling and always thinking. When she heard what sounded like good advice on mining amid the drunken ramblings, she slipped away from the bar to her back room and jotted notes about what the miner had said. These unintentional tips and her own excellent business sense led her to several highly successful mining investments.

When the Kinseys arrived at the Forks, they built a cabin. They filed a claim on nearby Gold Hill, one of several rolling, sloping hills characteristic of the land from Dawson out to

If one had a gun, ammunition and time, hunting could help pay the bills. A moose or caribou could feed a family all winter, or the meat could be sold for $1 to $1.50 a pound.

Duck hunting was a pleasant way to obtain a Sunday dinner but, more important, it provided a little relaxation away from the claims.

the claims. Bonanza Creek and the Grand Forks Hotel were situated in a small, winding valley. Gold Hill, part of the informal town of Grand Forks, sloped up from the hotel and was quickly dotted with cabins and hillside claims.

The Kinseys set up their studio in a tent and began dividing their time between working their claim and photographing other miners working theirs.

Many miners felt that building a cabin was a waste of time when they could live out of a tent and continue working the ground, but the Kinseys were not there just to look for gold.

Despite the expense in time and money of building a cabin, the other alternatives to a tent were not attractive. A night at the Grand Forks or one of the best Dawson hotels ran as much as $12, but for those unable to afford the price of Klondike luxury, cots were always available in tents for as little as 50 cents a night. To rent one of the few available cabins cost almost as much—$100 a month. Roomers could eat at a restaurant, but that, too, could become prohibitive: a steak dinner cost $5 and a pork or lamb chop supper was nearly as much. However, butchered meat, when available, was cheaper than restaurant meals, and a moose or caribou shot in the summer provided food for an entire family until the following spring. A fifty-pound sack of flour lasted a long time but was still a hefty investment at $100. A family could defray costs by making a deal with a store or with a miner who shot a moose and sold part of the meat. When fresh meat was scarce, it brought as much as $1 to $1.50 per pound.

Liquor, however, was the item in greatest demand and highest in cost, averaging $50 a bottle. Cigars cost 50 cents each, cigarettes, $1.50 a pack and tobacco, $7 to $10 a pound. These high costs were due in part to the very unpopular tax imposed by the Canadian government on all liquor and tobacco brought into the country.

Winters in Dawson and Grand Forks were harsh and long. There were months of sub-zero weather, temperatures regularly dipped to -50° and -60° and supplies were often scarce. It is remarkable that not a single miner froze to death in Dawson that first winter of the gold rush.

There were deaths, although many less than would have resulted if it had not been for one of the first public services in the Klondike—a Catholic hospital in Dawson—which was supplemented soon after by the Good Samaritan Hospital, operated by the Presbyterian Church. Still, during the height of the rush, about one miner a month lost his life from a variety of maladies, ranging from heart attacks to pneumonia.

Scurvy was also a constant problem; fresh fruit and vegetables were more scarce than gold. Even potatoes grown in the Klondike cost $2 a pound. Dairy products were a rarity; milk was $30 a gallon and butter, $4 a pound when it could be obtained. Eggs cost $1 apiece and such imported packaged delicacies as oysters cost $25 for a one-pound tin.

There were schemes to beat the high costs, of course. Some were large-scale investments by far-sighted individuals like Belinda Mulrooney and Joe Ladue. But there were entrepreneurs at every level. Others made up for what they lacked in financial resources with a flair for creativity.

One young man had a novel approach to the

A Klondiker with a cow was a rarity, and he could do quite a business selling dairy products. But the animals had to be herded over the Dalton Trail, and feed in the Klondike was not cheap—$400 a ton for hay.

high cost of food. When sugar was selling for 30 cents a pound, before the annual winter scarcity set in, he spent every dollar he had acquiring a sugar supply. A few months later sugar was selling for $2 a pound and he was selling homemade taffy at the bargain rate of $1 per package. He made a huge profit until he ran out of sugar.

Another would-be businessman, an unemployed mine laborer, noticed that there was one item that was not only reasonable, but *free:* matches. He began going from store to store, taking the free boxes of wooden matches off counters, and he soon had his wife and children doing the same. One by one, stores began running out. Within a few days the man had a great supply of matches and no store seemed to have any for its customers.

The man was about to become a match merchant when he asked just one more storekeeper about the availability of matches. The merchant was irate, saying he was tired of putting matches out all week long only to have them disappear so quickly. The young businessman was happy with his apparent success until he found out that the storage shed behind the store was stacked from floor to ceiling with cases of matches.

What appeared to be a comical scene was closer to tragedy than it might seem. The man was not alone in his unemployment. He had no claim to work, only a hungry family to support. Many unsuccessful miners could not afford to leave the Klondike when they wanted, and often they had to look for work through the slow winter, booking passage home the following spring if they could raise the cash. And cash was often impossible to obtain. For those who could

The Kinseys staked their claim on Gold Hill. It wasn't a particularly rich claim, but they earned enough to pay expenses, keep several men working and still have a little gold to show for it all. Clarke is at the far left and Clarence is next to him. Clarke, as can be seen from his attire, spent more time in town and with the camera, while Clarence shoveled and supervised the mining.

Clarke and Mary's cabin was a wood-frame building typical of the turn-of-the-century homes in and around Grand Forks—small but comfortable. Clarence is seated at left; Clarke is standing.

From left, Klondikers George Archer, Bob Roberts and Clarke and Clarence Kinsey look over recently processed photographs at Grand Forks.

Out back at the Kinseys'. Mary and Clarke usually dressed as if they were in the Seattle area. Mary is holding Dick, a Newfoundland pup that was a Kinsey pet for years. Clarke's watch fob was made from gold taken from his Gold Hill claim. The part of the cabin to the right of the doorway was the storeroom, where meat was kept refrigerated by the winter weather.

get a loan from another miner, the interest rate was steep—ten percent on a ten-day loan. But the only ones who could borrow money were those who had collateral, and matches certainly didn't suffice.

Clarke and Clarence Kinsey went to the Klondike better prepared than most. They had an adequate bankroll to finance their trip and to pay their expenses once they arrived. More important, they didn't expect to rely on their luck at finding gold. With their photographic equipment the Kinsey brothers were able to earn a respectable living at their trade. They did a substantial amount of portrait work as well as spending a good deal of time along the streams. Miners were anxious to have their pictures taken to send home to families and friends to let them know they were all right and as keepsakes of their time in the Klondike.

The Kinseys' gold claim was not a big producer, but the fact that it even paid its way put it in the minority. Still, after working the claim, buying photographic supplies and photographing their peers, the Kinseys worked almost four years before they could afford to move their studio into a permanent wood-frame building. They worked out of a tent at the Forks and out of a smaller one when they traveled up and down the creeks, recording the mining activities.

There was as great a demand for written news as there was for photographs, and dozens of publications sprang up almost overnight. Most appeared only a time or two before disappearing, but several—such as the *Klondike Nugget* and the *Dawson Daily News*—became northern institutions.

The Kinseys' photos appeared in the *Daily News,* several other short-lived publications and in brochures and pamphlets advertising goods for the miners and describing the Klondike for Outsiders.

The fact that the Kinseys paid their own way, owned a cabin, operated a producing gold mine and even employed a third young man, Al Johnson, as a photo assistant never made them rich, but by Klondike standards it spelled success.

Archer, Clarence and Asa Thurston Hayden, whose sketches were well-known in the Klondike and appeared in such publications as the Dawson Daily News.

The Loneliness of the North

In addition to the high prices of the Klondike there was a greater problem—loneliness. Most of the miners looked long years for gold, and those who didn't probably felt as if they had. The looking was as mentally taxing as it was physically demanding. The actual mining was extremely strenuous work, and for the vast majority of the men it was a solitary life. In most cases families and friends and wives and sweethearts were thousands of miles away. Life was very difficult for those who found gold, almost unbearable for those who didn't.

There were dance hall girls in the saloons who earned a better living than most miners by providing companionship over a bottle and on a dance floor. Some supplemented their income by continuing to provide companionship through the night. But many didn't need to, since they earned enough just drinking and dancing, and there were prostitutes to pick up where the dance hall girls left off.

But out along the claims where there were no women, just long hours of hard work and cold weather, dogs became the alternative to human companionship, and miners were willing to pay even more for a mutt than they would for a woman. The dogs could be expensive; even before the rush began in earnest, dogs were hard to come by. They were a necessity to pull sleds at first and later they were, indeed, a man's best friend. At times they were a man's only friend. Arthur Perry, one of the miners who had toiled for years in the North, joined the eastward exodus from Alaska when gold was discovered

The Kinseys' "caption" on this photo tells the story for many of the Klondike miners.

Klondikers needed a break from the months of hard work, and the spring cleanup was just the excuse they needed to celebrate the end of a long winter.

in the Klondike. He had been prospecting near Circle City when word reached him of the strike everyone had expected for years. After reaching the Klondike, he wrote to a friend in Juneau:

> *About March 15th, 1897, I reached the diggings from Circle City having hauled my sled the whole distance without a dog. The importance of the new strike had become too significant to be overlooked, and about 300 men from Circle City undertook the journey in mid-winter. Such an exodus was never known before in the history of the Yukon, but not a man lost his life, although several had their faces and toes nipped at times. Even some of the most resolute and dissolute women made the journey in safety. Fancy prices were paid for dogs by those who were able to purchase, and as high as $175 and even $200 were paid for good dogs. Almost any kind of dog was worth $50 to $75 each.*

That was only the beginning of the high prices and the high hopes. Perry went on, "When I first reached the new camp I was invited to go down [the] shaft and pick a pan of dirt." The diggings to which he referred were the streams surrounding Grand Forks; the shaft was on three Eldorado Creek claims owned jointly by Clarence Berry, a fruit farmer from Fresno, California; Antone Stander, a sheep herder from Austria; and James Clements.

"To my surprise," Perry said of his first pan of dirt in the Klondike, "it was $282.50. In fourteen pans of dirt they took out $1,565 right at the bottom of the shaft." That shaft measured only four feet by eight feet and was no more than a thawed column through the soil down to the paystreak just above bedrock.

Berry and Stander were regulars at the restaurant and bar in Belinda's hotel, and their claims turned out to be some of the richest ever staked in the Klondike. Although they were offered $500,000 for them in 1897, they refused without hesitation.

What Perry had seen in gold was remarkable even by Klondike standards, but in terms of dogs, it was only the beginning. It became common to buy and sell good dogs for $500, and it was not unusual for them to cost even more.

A dog was a companion, a means of transportation and in winter a potential lifesaver—a guide to safety or a living blanket in a snowstorm. And because of this, dogs ate as well or better than their owners.

Even in hard times a miner could buy himself a plate of beans and bacon for 25 cents; but a rice-meal dinner for a malemute might cost several times as much. However, if that was what the dog liked, that was the meal it got.

In many instances a miner would buy a dog only to find out that it was of little use as a working animal, but he would still pay hundreds of dollars to keep it fed and healthy as a pet.

Perhaps the most impressive dog in all of the Klondike was a Saint Bernard named Nero. He belonged to Belinda, who took him from an engineer who could not afford to feed him, and she and the powerful dog, said to be the largest in the territory, became a common sight on the trail between Grand Forks and Dawson. In winter Belinda rode on a sled drawn by Nero, all by himself.

Belinda had a reputation for showing compassion for animals during her years in the North. She once said of her trips into the Klondike that the passes were hard on everyone—men, women and especially animals. "The cruel wind would tear the flesh off their faces," she said of the pack animals. She made bonnets for the horses and dogs, and on at least one trip, rubbed ointment on the animals to heal the wounds that opened up.

But it was Nero who was Belinda's pride and joy. One spring when Belinda left on a business trip to Seattle she had one of her employees keep Nero tied up in Dawson until her boat left. She boarded a steamer and was on the first few minutes of the long journey Outside when miners aboard noticed an animal on the shore running parallel to the ship.

Once he got several hundred feet ahead of the bow, the dog leaped into the water and began swimming toward the boat. The miners cheered when they realized it was Nero, calling to the captain to stop. He refused, fearing the boat would be caught in the strong current and dragged into shore. But the miners were insistent and the captain relented. The boat stopped—without mishap—and the miners hauled the dripping dog on board and took him to Belinda's cabin. She took Nero to Seattle with her, booking two rooms in a hotel—one for her and the adjoining one for Nero. Nero was bathed and fed, and his stay in Seattle was as comfortable as any hotel guest's.

It was one of Belinda's customers at the Grand Forks Hotel who immortalized Nero for the rest of the world: Jack London used him as a model for Buck in *The Call of the Wild.*

Nero, Belinda Mulrooney's Saint Bernard, was said to be the largest dog in the territory.
(Reprinted with permission from *The Seattle Times*)

FAIRVIEW HOTEL.
OTEL OFFICE
FAIR VIEW
301

The Fairview Hotel

Despite her success at Grand Forks, Belinda was impatient. In just a year, she had accomplished what few thought she or anyone else could: she not only built a hotel, but an entire city, at least indirectly.

Profit was only one of her motivations; she also had an unbelievable ambition for singular success, the desire to accomplish what others could not.

So, as Grand Forks and the Grand Forks Hotel thrived, Belinda made plans to build another hotel—not just a better one, but the finest one in the Klondike, better than any of the new buildings in Dawson. She purchased a prime downtown lot in Dawson, which was growing even faster than Grand Forks, and put a crew to work on the new hotel, a three-story building.

Belinda single-handedly arranged the entire project and single-mindedly saw that it was done her way. However, the actual details of how she accomplished this were not fully disclosed until Belinda was in her seventies. Interviewed then, she recalled that she ordered all of the finest fixtures and supplies for the Fairview from Outside. When she went to supervise the packers hauling these things through the pass, she said she found that the team of men had apparently received a better offer to take a load of whiskey into Dawson, and so had abandoned her entire shipment halfway up the Chilkoot.

The Fairview, Belinda's second hotel, was the finest in the Klondike. (Courtesy of Mrs. Malcolm MacMillan)

Angry because she had paid for all the fixtures and their hauling in advance and had scheduled an official opening for the hotel, Belinda said she went into Skagway and confronted Soapy Smith, the hoodlum who controlled the city. Belinda said she demanded his help and received it. However, the facts and her recollections may have been tempered by the years and whether Smith was involved or not is only conjecture. Nevertheless, Belinda's supplies somehow reached Dawson on schedule and the Fairview opened as planned.

The Fairview measured 30 by 135 feet, had 30 steam-heated guest rooms, Turkish baths and a dining room where the tables were spread with linen and meals were served on bone china and the guests ate with sterling silver flatware. There were cut-glass chandeliers in the lobby (lights and bells were powered by a generator on a yacht anchored in the Yukon River) and an orchestra played chamber music. Belinda also had a private office in the Fairview and there was, of course, the bar.

Belinda had no patience with rowdy miners, and at both the Grand Forks and the Fairview, the clientele may not have been particularly well-dressed or well-educated, but they were clean and polite or they didn't stay long. Belinda demanded that from both her guests and her employees.

Belinda no longer worked behind her bar, staffing it instead with the type of educated men she preferred. These were often doctors and dentists from the States who had come to Dawson only to find that they were unable to practice immediately in Canada.

The night the Fairview opened, the bar took in $6,000. It was a financial success, to say the least, but even the Fairview, the finest hotel in the Klondike, had a flaw. The rooms—the first in the Klondike with brass beds and real sheets—were private, but the walls were just wallpaper glued to canvas that was stretched over wooden studding: the slightest whisper could be heard next door. If nothing else, the Fairview's walls taught the guests a great lesson in the need for discretion—and quiet conversation. Belinda also learned a lesson in investing at about the same time.

Belinda had agreed to split the costs of salvaging a beached freight barge in the Yukon with miner/businessman Big Alex McDonald in exchange for half of the goods on board. McDonald owned several claims in various parts of the Klondike, operating crews ranging from a handful up to as many as forty-five men on each of his stream and hillside operations.

But in Belinda's brief partnership with him, Alex got to the barge first and took half of the supplies, mostly food, and sold them at a huge profit. The other half of the salvage consisted mostly of water-damaged goods. Little was worth saving with the exception of a case of rubber boots, which Belinda stored for the summer, vowing to get revenge for what McDonald had done. The following spring, when McDonald's crews were idled by heavy rains, he went to her, remembering the boots. Belinda agreed to sell him the boots—for $100 a pair. He had to accept as it was the only way he could get his men back on the job.

Proper footgear, such as boots, was extremely important. Wet feet, even for the most dedicated miner, were more than an inconvenience. Toes could easily freeze during the best months of mining. Spring breakup usually didn't occur until April and the autumn frost set in as early as August. The shrewdness that caused Belinda to take a load of hot water bottles with her on her first trip into the Klondike paid off again when she salvaged the case of rubber boots from the freight barge.

Grand Forks

When Belinda opened the Grand Forks she had a monopoly; there were no other hotels in the area. But Belinda's success resulted in another rush: that of businessmen to the Forks.

By the time Belinda decided to move to Dawson and build the Fairview, Grand Forks had more than 1,000 residents. There were roughly 400 buildings in the town, mostly log cabins, but there were also a few wood-frame buildings. They all surrounded the forks of the streams where a little more than a year before there had been nothing but a single hotel and scattered miners' tents and makeshift cabins. Title to acreage along the creeks at Grand Forks was issued for the same $10 conveyance fee Ladue had paid at Dawson.

Dawson may have been the elegant metropolitan center Belinda sought, but someone else saw the town along the creeks as Belinda had seen it earlier. Max Endelman did not share Belinda's overriding desire for superiority, but he did share her ambition for wealth. He applied for title to more than a thousand feet of land along the main street—First Avenue—a 25-foot-wide dirt road along Bonanza Creek.

A very rough plan of the town was drawn up. Grand Forks was divided into ten blocks of up to two dozen lots each, with lot sizes and shapes varying considerably. Most miners were satisfied, however, simply wanting a lot on which to build a cabin; merchants wanted whatever size lots would accommodate construction of their stores, saloons and hotels so they could share in the business.

Endelman owned several dozen lots scattered over most of the blocks; each lot was large enough for several buildings.

Once the government had drawn up the rough plan, each lot and block was assigned a value and the land was sold to whomever applied for it. Lot prices ranged from $50 to $500, with most priced between $100 and $150. Cash was not needed, but the government charged a six percent annual interest rate on its real estate contracts.

If Belinda was known as the Queen of Grand Forks, Endelman could easily have claimed the title of king. Bonanza, as Grand Forks was called officially by the Canadian government, was mostly his. The town was generally considered as beginning at Claim Number 7 Above Discovery on Bonanza Creek and extending an unspecified distance upstream.

What Endelman hadn't obtained in early conveyances he purchased for the higher real estate prices. And when a title dispute came up over Endelman's ownership of Claim Number 6 Above Discovery on Bonanza Creek, which extended onto land the government felt should be reserved for a street, Endelman continued to turn to real estate rather than gold to make his Klondike fortune. He agreed to relinquish any claim to the mining rights of the land in question and to pay $2,500 to the Canadian government, in exchange for eleven and a half city lots in Blocks B and C—the two most valuable blocks in town, which surrounded the Grand Forks Hotel.

One of the early shots of Number 16 Eldorado. Tom Lippy, the owner, started the gold rush when he stepped off of the steamer Excelsior *in San Francisco with a suitcase weighted down with 200 pounds of gold on July 15, 1897. Two days later, when the* Portland *docked in Seattle with its load of Klondike gold, 5,000 people were lining the docks. The rush had begun. Clarence Berry and his wife were two of the passengers disembarking from the* Portland*, bringing out $130,000 in gold.*

Endelman also received an additional twelve and a half lots in two other blocks, and signed an agreement with the government promising not to resell the twenty-four lots for more than a total of $8,550, a figure the Canadian government determined would provide Endelman with ample compensation for his claim plus a reasonable profit. It was dealings such as these that kept the Kinseys and others on the nearby hillsides, where real estate values were lower.

Endelman began reselling these and his other lots, mostly to businessmen and women who wanted to be as near the center of town as possible. Cabins and stores were built on the other lots up and down the not-quite-parallel streets of Grand Forks.

Endelman didn't stop at undeveloped real estate, however. When Belinda decided to build in Dawson, Endelman was quick to react. Recognizing that she couldn't concentrate on making the Fairview Hotel the best, manage the Grand Forks and simultaneously keep on top of her growing list of mining properties, he made her an offer on the Grand Forks. Belinda sold the Grand Forks to Endelman and his partner, Bert Shuler, for $24,000.

Endelman nearly doubled the size of the hotel with a thirty- by fifty-foot addition. The main floor had a bar and restaurant, as before, as well as an office for the proprietor. The enlarged hotel had twenty-eight private guest rooms (still on two floors) and a large room for overflow guests, which was really nothing more than a vast open space with a row of cots onto which a miner could toss a bedroll and escape the cold.

Endelman also built another hotel, the Gold Hill, which he turned over to H.W. Leonard to manage for him. Leonard, a master of elegant dining, offered patrons a choice of chicken or turkey dinners in the hotel restaurant every Sunday. The Gold Hill even had a physician in residence, G.W. Elliott of Manitoba. His presence provided a potentially lifesaving alternative to the almost thirty-mile round trip into Dawson for a doctor in an emergency.

The town was growing more rapidly than even Belinda had guessed it would.

The Dewey Hotel, which Endelman later bought, and the Blanchard, Vendome, Butler, Garvie, Eldorado and Grand hotels were all built at about the turn of the century, and most were surprisingly well-built and well-furnished.

Alex Garvie owned the Garvie Hotel and Livery Stable. A former dairy farmer from Washington State, Garvie brought his own pack animals over the Dalton Trail. He believed that by bringing in his own supplies he could eliminate the middlemen and keep prices down.

Garvie's wife helped run the hotel and stable and was also the unofficial banker of Grand Forks. Currency was scarce and it was often difficult to find change. Mrs. Garvie kept rolls of bills stuffed in the tops of her stockings—tens and twenties in one; ones, twos and fives in the other. Whenever anyone needed change for a $100 bill or a gold piece, he or she headed for the Garvie. The proprietress would turn around, hike up the hem of her skirt and pull the change out of her stocking tops.

The Eldorado Hotel, owned by the Tardell brothers, and the Butler House, owned by George Apple and another ambitious Klondike businesswoman, Addie Butler, were both along First Avenue, near the Grand Forks.

The Gold Hill and the Dewey were across an unnamed lane that ran between First and Second

Grand Forks photographed from Gold Hill. The large building at left (with the General Merchandise sign) was John J. Healy's North American Transportation & Trading Company. The drug store across from the NAT&T belonged to Grand Forks mayor Walter Woodburn. The Kinsey studio was later built between Woodburn's and Coutts' tent stable in the foreground. Moving down First Avenue from there was the hotel district: the Northern, the Dewey, and Belinda's Grand Forks. The frozen trickle of water winding through the lower portion of the picture is Bonanza Creek.

NORTHERN HOTEL
DRUGS
CAFE
STABLES.

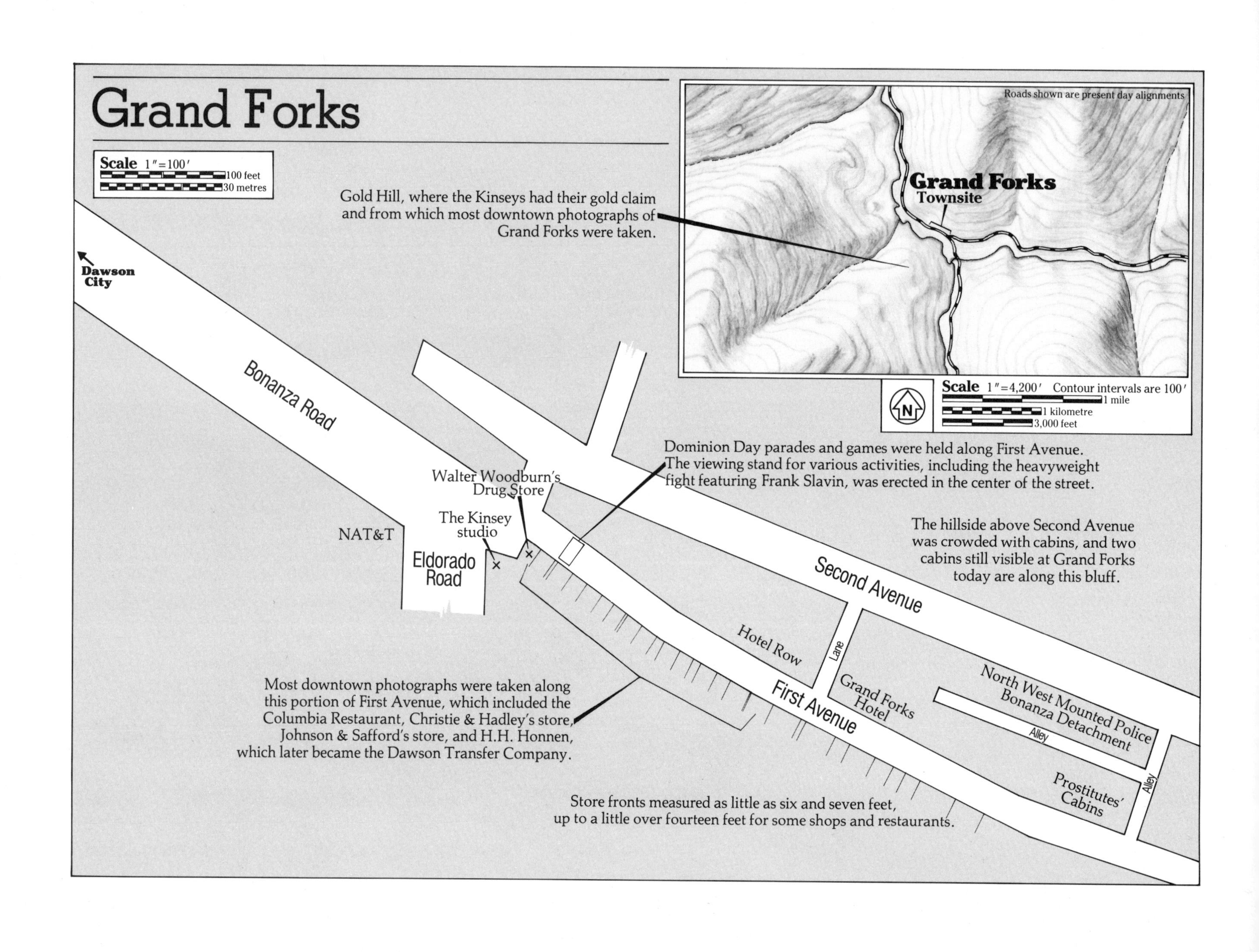
Grand Forks
Scale 1″=100′
100 feet
30 metres
Roads shown are present day alignments
Grand Forks
Townsite
Scale 1″=4,200′ Contour intervals are 100′
1 mile
1 kilometre
3,000 feet
N
Gold Hill, where the Kinseys had their gold claim and from which most downtown photographs of Grand Forks were taken.
Dawson City
Bonanza Road
Walter Woodburn's Drug Store
The Kinsey studio
NAT&T
Eldorado Road
Dominion Day parades and games were held along First Avenue. The viewing stand for various activities, including the heavyweight fight featuring Frank Slavin, was erected in the center of the street.
The hillside above Second Avenue was crowded with cabins, and two cabins still visible at Grand Forks today are along this bluff.
Second Avenue
Hotel Row
Lane
Grand Forks Hotel
North West Mounted Police Bonanza Detachment
Alley
First Avenue
Prostitutes' Cabins
Alley
Most downtown photographs were taken along this portion of First Avenue, which included the Columbia Restaurant, Christie & Hadley's store, Johnson & Safford's store, and H.H. Honnen, which later became the Dawson Transfer Company.
Store fronts measured as little as six and seven feet, up to a little over fourteen feet for some shops and restaurants.

avenues. The rest of the business district and the other hotels stretched out along Bonanza Creek. Buildings were constructed according to the availability of land and with no consideration to any informal town limits; in fact, the territorial government never established any precise boundaries for Grand Forks.

In addition to the hotels, which were by far the largest buildings in Grand Forks, there were also two blacksmith shops, one along First Avenue near the Grand Forks Hotel and one farther out along Bonanza Creek. Belinda owned a cabin near the Grand Forks, but a large portion of the rest of the block was vacant until after Belinda moved to Dawson.

One section of the block, stretching from First Avenue to Second Avenue, was reserved for a proposed North West Mounted Police detachment, something the Canadian government recognized as a necessity once the town began growing so rapidly. Also in the same block was a small saloon, the Bonnifield, which was between Belinda's cabin and the blacksmith shop. Several cabins lined First and Second avenues.

Farther downstream on Bonanza Creek, First Avenue jogged and intersected with Bonanza Road, which eventually led off toward the Ridge Road to Dawson. At the intersection, two almost perpendicular roads, Second Avenue and Eldorado Road, dead-ended into one another. The result was a large, almost diamond-shaped intersection of four streets, testimony to the impatience of the miners who first settled the town. This was just one of the peculiarities about Grand Forks which gave surveyors fits when they tried to turn the site into an orderly city.

Most Grand Forks merchants either had living quarters in their stores or in cabins nearby. These included druggists Frank Clark, Cribbs & Rogers, and Walter Woodburn, who was the unofficial mayor of the town; butchers Danuels & Watkins and the Barton Brothers, who were headquartered in Dawson and offered Dawson prices on meat and livestock at their Independent Market at the Forks; Morrison's laundry; freighters H.H. Honnen and Orr & Tukey; a public bath operated by Nita Brundage; an icehouse, also owned by Orr (the former mayor of Tacoma, Washington) and his partner; three barber shops; Coutts Livery Stable; and several bakeries, restaurants and general stores.

One of the downtown cabins belonged to two men—Giesman and Klienart, photographers. They and the Kinseys were by no means alone in their desire to photograph miners and mining in the Klondike. But most of the others in the area lived and worked out of Dawson.

For entertainment the Grand Forks hotels had bars with dancing and gambling, but the town did not have a theater; miners wanting stage shows had to go to Dawson, as they did for a library or bank, or a dentist or police officer—at least during the town's early years. However, even though there was no stage for her, Grand Forks did have at least one actress of some reputation. Max Endelman brought Violet Raymond to his hotel from Juneau, where she had been performing at the Opera House; Endelman did not bring her to perform, however. He lured her north with his talk of gold to become his mistress. She was quite an attraction, and most miners seemed quite content to sit and drink and just stare at her.

Overleaf: The upstream end of Grand Forks, looking the opposite direction from the photos on pages 40-41 and 44-45, also from Gold Hill. The Grand Forks Hotel is in the center and behind it, miners', workers' and prostitutes' cabins along Second Avenue, which ran roughly parallel to First Avenue.

BLACKSMITH
GRAND FORKS
MAY 2 1901.

ELDORADO
HOTEL

The photo at the left was taken at one of Frank and Clarence Berry's rich Eldorado claims. The two-story log cabin (left center) was one of the better-constructed in the Klondike. The above photo, a close-up of the cabin, typifies the Klondike miners' attitude—always time for fun despite the hard work. Clarence is at the left, playing the violin.

One night while Endelman was elsewhere, Antone Stander—tall, good-looking and younger than Endelman—approached Violet. He offered her gold dust and nuggets and a diamond necklace that was said to have reached to her knees. Such male dowries were quite common in the Klondike. One miner, for instance, found a young woman who was more than willing to marry him—but only after he gave her her weight in gold: 125 pounds.

Stander's offer was apparently enough for Violet. She said yes, and regardless of how Endelman felt about the incident, he never showed any emotion; he simply continued to concentrate on his business dealings.

Several miners tried ploys such as these with Belinda, but she was far too selective—and far too wealthy—to listen.

Stander married Violet, but he stayed closely involved with his claims, returning to the Klondike after a honeymoon Outside. After Stander and Clarence Berry bought out the third member of their group, they operated five sluices around the clock in spring and summer; they then split up their interests and ran even larger crews, sometimes forty or more men per claim.

Berry, unlike Stander, did not have to worry about luring a woman with his gold. He was already married when he arrived in the Klondike, and his wife worked the claims, too, cleaning up several thousand dollars in fine gold herself simply by working the spoil heaps adjacent to the sluices.

Despite incidents like the one between Endelman and Stander, there was a tremendous camaraderie among miners. Once the race to stake a claim was over, most miners were quick to help others when they could.

If a miner became ill or was injured on a claim outside of town, other miners had to carry him to the nearest cabin or hotel. The ambulance of the Klondike was a litter carried relay style from claim to claim. But if a miner died, there was more of a problem.

It was expensive to bury anyone, and if the dead person was indigent or if there was any question regarding foul play, the body had to be taken from Grand Forks to Dawson. There bodies were kept in a makeshift morgue—the North West Mounted Police Barracks—until an inquest could be held. Finally, when the stench became terrible, the Mounties moved the bodies into their blacksmith shop, which was also makeshift—a small shack built from an old wooden scow. It did not take long for the stench to overpower that small building, as well.

The police inspector asked that a morgue be built. He suggested a simple ten-foot by fourteen-foot building with a concrete floor and "a couple of slabs for bodies." It was never built. Instead, the government of the Yukon Territory advertised for bids in hopes of hiring a private mortician who could serve as coroner and also provide morgue space. Dawson eventually acquired an undertaker.

Grand Forks at least had a cemetery, although it was high above Bonanza Creek opposite Gold Hill. It was a long hike from town, especially with a body, but the cemetery was built so far from the town out of necessity. Any location in the valley would have subjected the bodies to the very distinct possibility of a rather rude extrication if gold were found nearby.

It was difficult and expensive to live in the Klondike, and not a whole lot simpler to die there.

Staking the Claims

In addition to the high costs of living and dying, there was also the high cost of mining, and mining was the reason most of the Klondikers were there. Every miner had to pay a $15 entry fee and a $100 annual fee just to begin looking for gold. Then came miscellaneous registration, filing, refiling and licensing fees—merely to mine and keep mining. If a miner got lucky enough to find gold, the tax man was there, too, taking a hefty royalty for the Canadian government, the percentage depending on how much gold was mined and in what period of time. This is one reason for the many discrepancies in the estimates of gold taken out of the Klondike during the gold rush and the years that followed. More than a few miners simply took their gold and left, preferring the risk of losing it or having it stolen to the certainty of taxes.

Once the miners paid their fees and were outfitted with supplies, they became part of a human stampede to the creeks. The rush to the streams from 1896 to 1898 had the potential for disaster but, amazingly, violence over staking was rare. The Canadian law forbidding sidearms in the territory probably saved even more lives than the law requiring each miner to have a year's supplies.

One of the first men to arrive after the rush and the staking began was William Ogilvie, a Canadian surveyor who had been in the North for years. He was sent out to Bonanza and Eldorado creeks before there was any hint of a town growing. With other government surveyors, Ogilvie worked up and down the streams until after Grand Forks began to grow. There was far more concern with making sure claims were measured correctly than with the width of streets in a mining town.

Surveyors such as Ogilvie worked frantically. More than 10,000 claims were filed in the Klondike before the end of 1898. It is not difficult to imagine that most miners were less than accurate in marking off their 500 feet of stream. Many claims were only 300 or 400 feet long simply as a consequence of the miners' haste. But if a miner was overzealous and marked off an oversize claim, he was legally required to forfeit the excess for open restaking. In some cases that could mean forfeiting the most valuable section of a claim.

Many miners followed the government surveyors on their rounds, gobbling up the fractional claims as soon as they were put back in the public domain. If a miner who was faced with losing a portion of his claim acted quickly, however, he could have an eligible friend, relative or partner refile for the fraction. This would assure the original owner of keeping the excess, unless of course, the new owner got greedy. Many unmarried miners were critical of the Canadian government for allowing married women to file claims. This was usually done so the husband could work an additional claim beyond the number allowed by the government, and obviously put unmarried miners at some disadvantage.

These fractions could be as valuable or

worthless as any other claims. Perhaps the most famous fraction belonged to a miner named Dick Lowe, once an assistant to Ogilvie. Lowe is reputed to have taken $500,000 in gold from his pie-shaped claim at the junction of Bonanza and Eldorado creeks and Big Skookum Gulch. On its widest side, the claim was only 86 feet long.

Not surprisingly, one of the most successful miners—in fractions or full-size claims—was Belinda Mulrooney, whose business sense and good luck did not stop at hotel management.

Belinda purchased from Antone Stander half of Number 40 Above Discovery on Bonanza, and that was one of her richest claims. Number 26 Above, on the same stream, where Belinda supervised a crew of twelve, yielded $1,000 a day. She took over another Bonanza claim after it had been worked unsuccessfully for three years. The previous owner had worked only 75 feet of the claim, so Belinda abandoned that portion of Number 57 Below and put a crew to work on another section, where a rich seam of gold was discovered on what had been thought to be a worthless mine simply because it had not been developed properly.

Belinda also had claims on Dominion and Eldorado, plus several bench claims. Her most impressive mining effort was not these individual claims, however, but an entire company. This was what made her a millionaire, her hotels and other claims making her only exceedingly wealthy.

Belinda and several partners took over the Gold Run Mining Company when it was losing money. She managed the company personally, and in eighteen months it showed a profit of $1.4 million. On one claim alone, Number 12 on Gold Run Creek, she ran a fifty-man crew.

When Belinda took over the Gold Run Mining Company there were far more problems than just low gold production. The owners operated a roulette wheel for employees, and stolen gold from the company coffers was being won—and lost—at the wheel. Belinda replaced it with a bridge table. She also saw that there were no more female camp followers hanging around, and fired the foreman, supervising the crews herself.

"I like mining," she told the *Dawson Daily News*, saying that she preferred to run a mine herself. "I only hired a foreman because it looks better to have it said that a man is running the mine, but the truth is that I look after the management myself." In a time when few women Outside had many rights, Belinda was telling men what to do, pacing up and down her claims, dressed in knee-high calfskin boots from New York and riding breeches covered with a short skirt.

Belinda knew how to get the most from her crews, just as she did from most of her investments. She demanded hard work, but she paid for it. She gave her men as much as $500 a month in bonuses for top production, an unheard of sum in a time when laborers were earning $1 an hour for shoveling dirt into sluices.

One newcomer marveled at how much Belinda had accomplished in the Klondike and how women in the East should have heard about her. "I'm just old-fashioned," she said. "And they wouldn't like it if they knew I sold liquor." Besides selling it, some people claimed that she smuggled it as well, bringing untaxed bottles into Canada in specially sewn canvas pouches in the lining of her fur coat.

By 1899 most miners were using steam points (thin pipes used to "point" steam into the frozen ground to thaw it). Steam points are visible in the foreground of this photo of a mine on Eldorado Creek. The steam pipes and pumps quickly replaced bonfires and were usually powered by small (fifteen-horsepower) boilers. Dirt was shoveled into the small ore cars and hauled back up to the top of the sluices for washing out.

Previous page: Gold Hill, viewed from the bluff above Grand Forks, was as busy as the streams below but required more work because miners working on the hill either had to haul water up to wash out their diggings or carry the diggings down to the stream. Property was cheaper on the hill, and it was dotted with cabins and other buildings soon after Grand Forks became more than a tent town. The hillside claims produced gold, but never in the quantities of the streams below.

In addition to becoming wealthy through hotel construction and management and through her many mining interests, Belinda did much for the Klondike. While she earned her own fortune she made the communities of Grand Forks and Dawson better places to live and work.

The *Dawson Daily News* summed up Belinda's accomplishments in 1899, noting among other things that she was "the main promoter of the telephone lines in the city, buying out a competitor and seeing that the one remaining phone line was stretched to Grand Forks and Dominion." Beyond that, she was a partner in the Hygiea Water Company, and the prime force in getting clean water for drinking and bathing so Dawson residents did not have to rely on boiling melted snow. The newspaper went on to say that she was "a woman of remarkable energy. She possesses a business foresight that would do credit to any businessman. She has . . . outstripped those of the sterner sex who have connected with large business enterprises on the Outside. Faith and daring are not wanting in her plans for all future operations. She stands without rival as the most successful woman of the Klondike in mining, hotel management and other large enterprises."

Belinda continued not only with her excellent business planning, but with her good luck as well. In 1899 a large fire ripped through Dawson, nearly leveling the business district. It took volunteer fire fighters nearly ten minutes just to get the first water on the blaze. The fire destroyed 117 buildings and caused an estimated $1 million in damage. But the Fairview was not harmed. The hotel's lobby became a refuge for scores of tired and suddenly homeless Klondikers. Men and women slept in two-hour shifts in the lobby while the rebuilding process began almost before the ashes had cooled.

After the fire, Dawson was stunned but by no means destroyed. Belinda went to work with other leaders planning a more permanent town. Many of the buildings lost in the fire had been poorly constructed, but their replacements were built with an eye to the future, as Belinda had done when she built her Grand Forks and Fairview hotels.

Fire escapes were added to new buildings and to the ones left standing. They were added in Grand Forks as well, since the threat of fire there was as great as in Dawson. From then on, ladders ran along the roofs of buildings and down the sides; most ladders were wooden, but some building owners managed to have metal ones shipped north. In some buildings, skylights were added as additional escape routes.

The 19th century was over and the Klondike was entering the 1900's with a definite look of permanence. In Grand Forks and in Dawson, streets, buildings, sewers and public services were upgraded. Clarke and Mary Kinsey began the new century with a trip Outside for the birth of their first child, Leonard. And as the 20th century began, Belinda was seriously involved romantically for the first time since she had come into the territory almost three years earlier. The Klondike gold area was approaching its most glorious years.

—III—

The Peak Years

The new century, more than just a chronological milestone, represented a monumental change in the Klondike for many reasons. The 20th century ushered in a sense of permanence in the Klondike mining district—a great transition from a hustling, growing gold rush era to a more settled civilization that extended from Dawson to Grand Forks and out along the streams. Mining was becoming mechanized, and it was an era of gold production rather than gold seeking.

The White Pass & Yukon Route railway had eliminated the life-and-death struggles over the passes, and the discovery of gold in Alaska at a place called Nome took away a great deal of the transient element.

One more important event took place; Belinda Mulrooney found an elegant, stylish gentleman who could lure her at least far enough away from her far-flung enterprises for a down-home courtship.

Charles Eugene Carbonneau, who had arrived in the Klondike on August 30, 1899, made a grand entrance. He passed out small, finely printed business cards bearing his name, title (he called himself a count) and the companies he represented. He was a salesman, specializing in only the finest French champagnes.

Carbonneau was attracted to Belinda as soon as they met, and she became the target of his most persuasive sales efforts. Belinda, too, was

Nationalities were unimportant when it came to celebrating holidays in the Klondike. Although the Union Jack suggests that these miners from out along Sulphur Creek may have been British subjects, they were nevertheless getting ready to head for Grand Forks and the 1902 Fourth of July festivities.

Belinda and Charles Eugene Carbonneau. He claimed to be a count, although one miner swore he recognized him as a barber from Montreal, and the circumstances concerning his death in Europe during World War I were never quite clear.

(Reprinted with permission from *The Seattle Times*)

enthralled. The count wore a monocle and spats and was seldom seen without his personal valet. He began sending Belinda a bouquet of roses every day and soon the two were seen together almost constantly.

Despite the fact that a French-Canadian working on Tom Lippy's crew swore that he recognized the count as a barber from Montreal, Belinda accepted Carbonneau's marriage proposal.

Belinda had electricity installed in Dawson's Saint Joseph Church for her evening wedding ceremony, ending a year-long courtship. But several disgruntled miners who were disappointed that Belinda had chosen anyone (let alone the count), pulled the plug—literally—on the wedding. After a slight delay for candles to be lit, the ceremony continued and the following day the newlyweds boarded a steamer out of Dawson for the first leg of their long honeymoon journey to Paris.

During their several-week stay in Paris, the Carbonneaus were a familiar sight along the Champs Elysees in their coach, which was drawn by two huge white horses in jeweled harnesses. Whenever they stepped from the coach, an Egyptian footman unrolled a long red carpet from the carriage to whatever doorway they were entering. But Belinda was certainly not finished with the Klondike; after their honeymoon, the Carbonneaus returned to the Yukon Territory and Belinda and the count jointly managed her mining interests. The Klondike was at its peak in virtually all respects.

Besides the Carbonneaus, there were roughly 10,000 permanent residents in Dawson, 4,000 persons in Grand Forks and another 5,000 living out along the creeks surrounding Grand Forks. It was difficult to make a precise count, since there were still miners coming and going frequently, and undoubtedly there were many who were never counted—or perhaps were counted twice—but unlike the gross estimates of a few years earlier these figures fairly accurately portrayed the Klondike.

Of the 4,133 Grand Forks residents who lived within the vague boundaries from Number 7 Above on Bonanza, up the hillsides and along Upper Bonanza, 3,727 were men; 283 were women and 123 were children. Beyond Bonanza Creek, the population along the streams was even more male-dominated—4,904 men, 266 women and 140 children. The women in town were probably an even mixture of prostitutes, shopkeepers and housewives. Out along the streams, most of the women were housewives, with the exception of a few who were mining (most of whom were probably widows) and a few who were operating roadhouses or stores.

The Canadian government had a lot more to face with this new century's settled population than it had had with the thousands of semi-crazed miners inhabiting the creek banks. The federal and territorial governments had viewed the gold rush as a gigantic but temporary problem. But when the miners began building homes, churches and communities instead of leaving, the problems grew. The people needed services, not just a police force. And public services lagged far behind private ones. The Dawson water and telephone utilities that Belinda had helped organize, for example, were both private enterprises.

Thanks to Belinda's earlier efforts, phone service cost no more in Grand Forks than in Dawson; the price a flat rate of $30 per month.

Calls between Grand Forks and Dawson cost subscribers $1, regardless of the length of the call. The general public could use the lines, too, but the toll was $1.50 for nonsubscribers.

There were enough subscribers to the telephone service—125—to warrant the Klondike's first telephone directory. Seventy-two of the phones were in Dawson, with the rest distributed in and around Grand Forks. The telephone company, which had as much trouble defining town boundaries as the government, listed Grand Forks as having seventeen phones, with an additional nineteen at Bonanza, apparently referring to those connections outside of the main business district but still nearby.

There were six phones along Eldorado, with the remaining eleven scattered farther out along the other creeks in the area. The phone book for Dawson even listed eleven general merchants, eight grocery stores, seven physicians, six attorneys, five hotels, five saloons, two bakers, one photographic studio and the undertaker, Frank Lowe, who divided his time between his mortuary and his furniture store.

The Grand Forks list of merchants was growing, too. More small shops were opening and, in addition to its doctor, the town had a dentist, Edward Volen Cabbage. Tooth extractions were free—one of the few things in the area that was. But there was a catch: *painless* extractions cost $1. And in the land of gold, gold crowns cost $10 each.

Grand Forks also had a library. When the privately owned Standard Circulating Library of Dawson became overstocked after receiving a shipment of 1,500 new books in 1900, the owners decided to open a branch out at the Forks. While there was no charge for reading books in the libraries, it cost three cents per day to check out a book, or a flat fee of $1 per month for an unlimited number of books.

But it was the addition of one major merchant that spelled permanence for Grand Forks. John J. Healy's North American Transportation & Trading Company—the NAT&T—opened large warehouse and retail facilities in town. The main store was in the same building as the Barton brothers' butcher shop; the warehouse was a few hundred feet down Bonanza Creek.

At the same time, William Ogilvie, who had risen from surveyor to commissioner of the Yukon Territory, no longer had to deal simply with mismeasured streets and claims, but with the much greater problem of a mismeasured territory. He found himself faced with seeing to the orderly development of the entire Yukon—from postal service to a school system to fire protection and more.

Much of what Grand Forks received in public services was as a stepchild of Dawson. The government would anguish over decisions for long months and then provide Dawson with what it needed, but six months late; Grand Forks would see results even later. For example, Dawson finally received adequate fire protection, but after its devastating million-dollar blaze of 1899, so did Grand Forks, some six months later still.

The Bonanza Detachment of the North West Mounted Police represented stability and permanence for Grand Forks. The unit was headed by Staff Sergeant Charles C. Raven and included a corporal, three constables and a special constable.

OFFICE
N W M P.
N W M POLICE
DETACHMENT GRAND FORKS Y.T.
KINSEY&KINSEY PHOTO

The territorial government determined that volunteer fire fighters simply weren't adequate, so a full-time territorial fire department was established, headquartered in Dawson. The branch detachment at Grand Forks was housed in a new building along First Avenue, and Bill Marshall of Nanaimo, British Columbia, was appointed the first fire chief. His new horse-drawn hook, ladder and chemical engine arrived in January 1900. Territorial firemen and the newly appointed territorial doctor at the Forks all earned the same wage—$150 a month.

Across the street from the fire station the lot reserved for the North West Mounted Police did not remain vacant for long. The new headquarters of the Bonanza Detachment was constructed on half of the reserved lot, facing Second Avenue. A lane ran between the police station and the other half of the lot, which faced First Avenue. The Mounties' new two-story wood-frame building measured about forty-seven by thirty-one feet. The main floor was partitioned off for officers' living quarters, a kitchen, a mess hall, a storeroom and a three-cell jail. The enlisted men's barracks was upstairs. A latrine, a sixteen-foot by twenty-foot stable and a lean-to for feed were adjacent to the main building. The detachment was headed by Staff Sergeant Charles C. Raven and included a corporal, three constables and a special constable.

The Mounties had little serious crime to contend with at Grand Forks. The most common offenses usually involved alcohol—drinking too much of it, selling it without a license, selling it to a dance hall girl, allowing a dance-hall girl to serve it, or being abusive, obscene or violent after drinking it. Most of those who were arrested simply slept it off in one of the three jail cells. If formal charges were filed, the accused man or woman was tried in Dawson in territorial court and usually received no more than a small fine.

There were occasional robberies, and most of those were also related to drinking. Many miners accused dance hall girls or prostitutes of stealing a poke of gold after an evening's entertainment, but more often than not the miners were the guilty ones—guilty of excessive drinking and spending.

In the turn-of-the-century Klondike, the Mounties were called upon for far more than law enforcement, and were valuable to the community mainly for their nonpolicing activities. They delivered mail locally and on fortnightly patrols throughout the Yukon; they served as timber and land agents when none were available to register land titles and issue permits for wood cutting; they served as government mining inspectors to accept new claims; and, perhaps most important, they were heroes to the children of Grand Forks.

It was the Mounties who built a wooden framework around a lot by the fire station so the fire hoses could be used to flood the lot in winter for an ice skating rink. And it was the Mounties who were the sports stars of the day. The territory went so far as to send its finest hockey players—a team composed of Mounties—to play the best eastern Canadian amateur teams. The results were inevitable: the Yukon team lost by lopsided scores, but the existence of the team emphasized to the rest of the country that the Yukon and the Klondike were permanent. The team gave the local children a group of athletes they could look up to.

This 1903 photo is typical of the early 20th century Klondike; many of the successful owners only visited their claims to pick up their gold—or to pose for portraits such as this. It was always easy to distinguish the workers from the owners by their attire.

Growing Up in the Klondike

The children of the territory, especially those outside of Dawson, did not have much to keep them entertained. The Yukon government established a school system for those aged seven to eighteen. After a census was taken, five schools were built in Dawson for the 175 school-age children. Rural "assisted" public schools were opened in each area outside of Dawson that had at least six school-age children. These were Grand Forks, Sulphur, Dominion and Granville, all of which had schools operated on the same strict guidelines as those in Dawson.

Most of the teachers were from eastern Canada, and all were certified public school teachers. They received the same wages as territorial firemen and doctors, $150 a month.

The schoolhouse at Grand Forks was austere but functional. The one-room building was built on Gold Hill and one teacher served all the children. Attendance fluctuated, ranging from a dozen students to as many as twenty or more. Both in Dawson and at the creek schools attendance was remarkably good, perhaps because there was little else for the children to do, especially in the coldest months of winter.

A territorial inspector made frequent visits to the schools, and the district was not above dismissing, or at least not rehiring, a teacher if students were not progressing adequately. Typical turn-of-the-century criteria were used in evaluating the progress of students and the effectiveness of teachers: no obscene writing on the walls, students situated so the sunlight shone over the proper shoulder while they worked and, of course, discipline. Teachers were required to be organized and keep their students well-behaved and motivated. A full curriculum was taught, including arithmetic and geometry, literature, Canadian and world history, physiology and reading, writing and English.

The Grand Forks teacher was a Miss Keyes, who also had taught the primary students in Dawson. While the demands on her may not have been difficult at Grand Forks, she had fifty-nine students to contend with when teaching in Dawson.

According to the territorial supervisor, Miss Keyes, a graduate of the New Brunswick Normal School (class of 1888), was "an earnest, conscientious teacher . . . endeavoring to do good work." But the supervisor was critical of her handling of the large number of students in Dawson; he felt that she was more suited to smaller groups of children.

> *. . .she has received no special training in primary work and is not ingenious in devising methods for engaging the attention of the class or stimulating their interest. . . . The smaller pupils should have work of varied kinds so they would never become wearied as they do when they are given the same process to repeat a great number of times. . . .*
>
> *In Phonics and reading the main principles are followed but there are very few devices used, and the teacher does not put the necessary amount of vim into this work and therefore fails to obtain in*

return the enthusiasm of her class. She would do much better in a room where [the students do] not require such versatility [and where there are] modern devices to arrest and retain the attention of the class.

Beyond the day-to-day school routine, there were few activities designed specifically for the younger Klondike residents. Most evenings the choices were homework, helping at their parents' stores or running errands. However, on Friday and Saturday evenings there were spelling bees, debates, dances or dinners for the children, alternating between Reverend Cook's Presbyterian Church and Reverend Comyn Ching's Anglican Church.

Many of the children were able to earn good wages if they worked in their spare time. The best-paying customers, those in the two high income businesses of Klondike society, were the miners and the prostitutes.

The miners were always hungry for news, and a paper route in the Klondike was very profitable. Any news from Outside, no matter how dated, was valuable. The youngsters would pick up newspapers as soon as they came into town, either at the Bonanza Newsstand or at Charles Bell's stage office, which also served as a news agency for Outside papers.

The boys borrowed horses if they were lucky,

Clarence and Agnes Kinsey's daughter Olive with Dick, the family dog. He originally belonged to Clarke and Mary, but became Olive's constant companion and would eat almost anything she fed him, including pickles, which he loved even though they made his eyes water.

or rented them from a stable to take papers out to miners along the creeks. The prices the miners were willing to pay for news more than covered the rental of the horses and the money the boys had to pay for the papers.

Children didn't have a lot to do in the Klondike, but like children everywhere, they usually found something to keep themselves busy. This steam thawer, which replaced the more primitive bonfires to thaw the Klondike ground, provided a perfect perch for these Klondike youngsters.

One of the boys, Jim Kingsley, also earned money hauling luggage for newcomers, at 75 cents a trip, and spent Sundays driving a two-horse stage out to Quartz Creek, earning $4 for the day's work.

Stable owner Alex Garvie was more than willing to rent the local boys horses for their work if he had them available. But when he caught three of the boys—Kingsley, Norman Nelson and Hugh Cutting—racing up and down the hillside instead of working, his cooperation ended abruptly.

But there was plenty for local youngsters to do on foot or with a dog team. While Belinda had seen to the establishment of a modern water supply for Dawson, there was no such thing in Grand Forks. So the boys with sleds hauled water into town during winter, when the creeks were frozen. The water still had to be boiled before it was used, but if snow from near the mines was melted, it had to be boiled, strained and then boiled again before it was fit to drink.

In winter it was much simpler for the townspeople to pay a quarter for a four-gallon bucket of fresh water from a creek or snowmelt outside of town. And for young Jim Kingsley, with his two-barrel sled and three dogs, hauling water was a good way to earn money and enjoy the countryside.

Still, the quickest way to make money was in town, and the girls as well as boys could share in the enterprise. The miners and prostitutes always needed someone to run errands. Men, while they were gambling, would send a boy out for cigars, tobacco or snuff, and the prostitutes had children bring packages from stores to their nearby cabins.

The Women of the Row

The prostitutes of Grand Forks easily could have walked up or down the street to pick up their own things, but these women occupied a very strange niche in Klondike society. They were accepted as a fact of life and part of the miners' society, but at the same time they were scorned if they crossed some mythical line into "legitimate" society.

Consequently, the prostitues went out of their way to avoid any needless confrontations. A few minutes' walk or run from the Row to a store and back usually brought the errand boy or girl a 50-cent piece as a reward and, to the girls' pleasure and boys' disgust, a kiss on the cheek.

On one occasion, ten-year-old Kingsley had the misfortune of receiving his tip—and kiss—in the middle of town directly in front of his father's Bonanza Clothing Store and Newsstand. It was more than he could take. In his embarrassment, he punched the woman in the stomach and ran. His father gave him a thrashing, explaining that regardless of the circumstances, a gentleman simply never punches a lady. Young Kingsley had to apologize to the understanding woman, and she paid him only in cash for future errands.

Businessmen like the elder Kingsley (who also ran a store several miles out of town on Bonanza) and most of the other men, whether they were frequenters of the prostitutes' cabins or not, had no objection to the women of the Row. It was the housewives who voiced whatever objections there were. Most of these women had been brought north by their husbands from a very different background and from larger communities, where prostitutes were never seen or heard from.

But in Grand Forks, the prostitutes' row of cabins was just across the street from the new North West Mounted Police headquarters. And next to the Mounties, the prostitutes were the adults the children admired most. The boys thought they were great, except for the kisses, and the girls thought they were beautiful.

Some of the women were, according to the local Mounties, "known prostitutes." Others who lived nearby probably were, but were left to entertain their customers while maintaining relative anonymity. Little was known about most of them unless they created a problem. For example, when prostitute Georgie Ryan was seen in the early morning at the Dewey Hotel, the police quickly stepped in. But the cabins that belonged to Fanny Feusht, Selma Saunders and Louise Plotstosher were, for all practical purposes, simply three more cabins just up the street from the one that belonged to Belinda Mulrooney Carbonneau. Few of the prostitutes were ever arrested or convicted of any crime, and in many cases the townspeople paid little attention to them. When one died of pneumonia, the town was amazed to discover that she had an estate worth $18,000, plus a share in a gold mine.

In another instance, one of the women made an unusually blatant intrusion on Grand Forks' social life. While the children had their evening spelling bees, the adults who didn't find saloons or dance halls to their liking had dances at a church or in the new social hall—a large one-room building with benches lining the walls. Parents could bring their children, who would sleep on the benches while the adults danced into the early hours of the summer mornings.

On one such occasion, a prostitute strolled through the front door and walked toward the center of the room. Finally, after several seconds of total silence, one of the wives stepped forward, told the guest that she was uninvited and asked her to leave.

The prostitute smiled, saying that she had been invited—by one of the men present, and if he would step forward and ask her to leave, she would be happy to do so. Apparently one of her customers had extended the invitation when he last visited her. Whoever he was, he didn't say a word and the prostitute just turned and left—and her unidentified customer was no doubt more than just a little relieved.

The interior of a Klondike parlor. This one was not quite as elegant as some, but much nicer than most. It did lack the trademark of the prostitutes' cabins: satin curtains.

The few encounters "proper" folks had with Klondike prostitution had its comical side, too. Before James Russell brought his family to Grand Forks from Whitehorse he purchased one of the cabins near the center of town. He had moved to the Forks earlier to take over the Vendome Hotel; then he sent for his family, which was still in Whitehorse, where he had managed the White Horse Hotel. He neglected to tell his wife that their dirt-floor cabin had formerly belonged to one of the town's young prostitutes. The only hint of furnishings that remained from the previous owner was a set of satin drapes on the small windows.

On the first night after Russell's family arrived, they were awakened by a loud knocking on the door. A very drunk man was insistent about coming in. Russell finally convinced him that the new residents were in a different line of work from the previous owner; he then had to be even more persuasive with his hysterical wife, who was horrified at the incident and the uncivilized town of Grand Forks, demanding that they leave.

Russell convinced his wife to stay, but he never could get her to believe that the working girls were harmless. His oldest child, Ethel, however, thought they were great fun. While her mother helped at the hotel, Ethel stayed at home and watched her younger brother and sister. She thought the young women who lived across the street were gorgeous, dressed in their fancy clothes. And they always waved and said hello to her when they walked by or when they sat in their doorways whiling away the daytime hours when business was slow. And, like the North West Mounted Police, the prostitutes always left gifts for the children of Grand Forks at Christmastime.

Klondike Holidays

Christmas was an important holiday in the Klondike, but it wasn't the most important. With little to do but work, Klondikers turned the few holidays they observed into glorious occasions. There was little celebrating in winter, with Christmas a relatively private, family holiday. It was simply too cold to go out and have a big public party. The children even had to abandon their ice skating in the worst months, when it was so cold that socks, shoes and skates—and occasionally feet—would freeze solid in only a few minutes, and any exposed skin would freeze even faster.

But in the spring and summer, Klondikers made up for lost partying time; picnics were common, with groups of anywhere from a single family up to a hundred or so people riding bicycles, taking carriages and walking to one of the bluffs above town for eating, singing and relaxation. Sometimes these parties were for a miner who had made the decision to sell his claim and take his cleanup Outside; then all his friends gave him a royal send-off.

After the long winter everyone was ready to blow off steam by the time the spring thaw rolled around in April, so April Fool's Day was an appropriate semiofficial first holiday of spring. One of the customary pranks was to nail a gold coin or intriguing-looking poke of dust to the boardwalk. Then everyone huddled inside nearby doorways until a Klondike newcomer spotted the treasure.

Sure enough his eyebrows would go up, he'd look over each shoulder to see if anyone could

The crowds in Grand Forks for Dominion Day, 1902, were surprisingly large. Most of the townspeople turned out for the festivities, as did many of the miners from areas farther out along the creeks. Competitions for children and adults included tug-o-war (seen here), horse races, bicycle races, sprints, long-distance races, weight-lifting and other events. (Courtesy of Yukon Archives)

see him and then greedily stoop to pick up the easy gold—only to be met by uproarious laughter. This was one of the local ways of welcoming naive newcomers. The children didn't miss out on the pranks, either. They would sit under a second-story hotel window in the evening and watch until they spotted a miner stagger toward his room after leaving one of the bars. They'd give him a few minutes to fall asleep and then cut loose with shouts of "Fire!" Inevitably someone would jump out a window before realizing what had happened.

May 24—Queen Victoria's birthday—was another excuse for putting work aside for a day, even though the majority of those in the Klondike were from the United States. When it came to holidays, nationalities were unimportant.

The real celebrations came in July, when there were several successive days of festivities. Little work was accomplished between July 1, Dominion Day, and July 4, Independence Day. Everyone—from mine owners and laborers, shop owners and clerks, Mounties and children—got into the act.

There were parades with Mounties from the territorial headquarters at Dawson's Fort Herchmer, from the Bonanza Detachment at the Forks and from other outlying posts. In Dawson there were indoor events at the Dawson Amateur Athletic Association building and baseball at the stadium. There were individual events for virtually everyone in both towns, and

All the proprietors decorated their buildings for Dominion Day. Olympia Beer was one of the most advertised in the Klondike, and it was available at Klondike prices: 25 cents a glass. Clarence, with his hand on the saddle, is in the picture at the left.

This celebration was a goodbye party for Jack Cannon who, with Charles Worden and the Stanley brothers, S.L. and William, was a partner in Numbers 24, 25 and 26 Eldorado. Cannon had decided to take his earnings and go home after the summer cleanup. The four men had been working a thirty-five-man crew all summer after unearthing a seam of gold in December. Miners seemed to revel in posing in odd places, as did the man in this photo poking his head through the chimney hole in the tent roof.

This photo was taken on Queen Victoria's birthday, May 24, on Dawson's waterfront, which was jammed with crowds preparing to move into town for the parade. The John C. Barr was one of Healy's North American Transportation & Trading fleet.

at the Forks, boxing matches were held in a ring surrounded by bleachers in the middle of town.

One year a fight featuring Klondiker Frank Slavin, who had been the heavyweight champion of the British Empire, filled not only the bleachers but also store fronts, streets and boardwalks at the Forks. But most of the events were for the men and children, with even a few for the women.

There were sprints and distance foot races, horse races, relay races, tug-o-wars, field events and more. It was a week when few miners worried about their claims. But it was also the 1900's and the rush was over. The claims were staked and there was not the hurry that had existed before. Waiting a week didn't mean missing out on any riches, only getting the gold out of the ground a few days later.

July 4, 1900, was also a day of celebrating throughout the Klondike—especially in Grand Forks and here in Dawson.

WELCOME
FRUITS
Fine Confectionery
SOFT DRINKS.
CIGARS & TOBACCO.

The 1902 Dominion Day celebrations included a heavyweight boxing match, which featured Frank Slavin, at one time heavyweight champion of the British Empire. The ring and this viewing stand, with bleachers (visible in the photo below), were set up in the middle of First Avenue, across the street from the Northern Hotel. The finish line for the races was also just below the stand.
(Courtesy of Yukon Archives)

ON & SWAN.
STATIONERY RETAIL.
CIGARS & TOBACCOS,
LIBRARY
DRUGS.
FRUITS
Fine Confectionery
SOFT DRINKS
CIGARS & TOBACCO
BONANZA NEWS
The New PORTLAND
Furnished Rooms
New York Store
GENTS FURNISHINGS

More Realistic Prices

With the new century, Klondike prices began to drop, steadily moving closer to at least bearable levels. Demand finally was slowing, while supply was beginning to increase. Prices never dropped to Outside levels, but they got closer than ever before.

Prices of most supplies and food dropped as much as forty percent a year after 1900. Butcher shops had large supplies of fresh meat and fresh fish was brought in regularly from Lake Laberge; scurvy, once rampant, rapidly disappeared.

Goods were brought in by steamer on the Yukon or overland by stage from Whitehorse. There never were unlimited supplies, but prices began to reflect a more realistic attitude in the Klondike; living was still expensive but the hectic pace and general impatience had slowed somewhat. Most consumers were willing—and able—to wait until the next shipment if the product they wanted was out of stock.

In Grand Forks at places like the NAT&T or shops such as Christie & Hadley's or the Gold Hill Store, clothing and household and mining supplies were still expensive, but more reasonable than the year before. Women could buy printed fabric or muslin to do their own sewing for 12½ cents a yard and shoes, in the latest styles, cost $2.50 a pair. Men's French cordovan leather shoes were $4.50 a pair. When it came to the necessities for working the claims, overalls were $12 a dozen, flannel shirts 75 cents each and long underwear $1.75 a set. And one necessity—Canadian Club whiskey—was considerably less expensive than before, but still $3.50 a bottle, or several times the Outside price.

A ten-mule freight team arriving in Grand Forks. This section of First Avenue was where the shipping district turned into the hotel district. Also at this end of the street were two drug stores (Walter Woodburn's and Frank Clark's); Charles Bell's newsstand; several bakeries and restaurants, including German, Austrian and Japanese eateries; a second-hand store; a jewelry store; a shoe repair shop; and the confectionary, which also housed the Grand Forks branch of the Dawson Standard Circulating Library.

PERCENTAGE AVENUE. GRAND FO

Transportation

The turn of the century ushered in favorable changes in prices, but the same could not be said for the roads over which goods traveled, at least not for several years. And as for the streets and boardwalks in Grand Forks, they could be downright hazardous—especially for youngsters and drunks.

In some cases, the boardwalks had been built far enough off the streets so that spring runoff and winter snowdrifts could accumulate under them, which presented dangerous drops of several feet. After the prostitutes, the boardwalks were one of the serious dangers Grand Forks mothers warned their children to avoid.

The Yukon Territory imposed a speed limit on its streets: horse or dog teams were not allowed to exceed six miles per hour and few did, since only a small number of the roads presented potential lawbreakers with the opportunity. First and Second avenues and adjoining Bonanza and Eldorado roads were the only streets in Grand Forks where horse and wagon traffic could operate comfortably.

The roads were most navigable in winter since they were frozen solid. The muddy streets dried out during the brief summer, but they were knee-deep in mud during the spring thaw and the autumn snows and rains.

Spring breakup brought more than just water for sluicing. It turned the roads in Grand Forks into mud two to three feet deep. Boardwalks helped, but for anyone who wanted to cross the street, there was no alternative but to wade through the mud.

To eliminate the hazardous ruts and potholes, mine tailings were used to fill the streets periodically, which proved little better than no fill at all, since the tailings consisted of washed-out dirt, gravel and rock and they tended to sink or wash away fairly quickly. At least alleys, lanes and hillside roads were not heavily traveled, and they were adequate for foot and some wagon traffic.

The government road (Ridge Road) from Dawson to Bonanza was the Klondike thoroughfare, running from downtown Dawson out across the Klondike River, up Bonanza and along Bonanza Road into downtown Grand Forks. This road followed the hillsides, so it was out of the way of the placer mining along the creeks and sheltered from drifting snow in winter. The Ridge Road had always been busy. An early correspondent for *Century* magazine followed the road out to the claims in 1897, soon after it was pioneered. He described it then as "a miserable excuse for a path, leading over rough hummocks, up hills and over bogs, through sticky, oozy muck, by brambles and bushes, across creeks and corduroy paths." And he was right.

The corduroy paths he referred to were the early attempts at paving. Rough-hewn lumber and logs were laid across the width of the road to cover some of the muck and ooze and to support the weight of wagons carrying supplies to the Forks. The government did little to upgrade

The Robertson stage used a six-horse team to haul this load of miners into Dawson from Grand Forks. There were at least a dozen riders outside the stage and probably as many inside. If a miner paid and could fit on board, he could ride.

the road during the next several years, except to dump a load of gravel in a particularly bad spot occasionally. But constant use finally wore a fairly respectable—and passable—path through the underbrush.

During the spring as many as 150 wagons were on Ridge Road at one time, and that figure never declined with the passing of the gold rush years; instead, the number grew as more and more freighters served Grand Forks and the creeks, bringing heavier and heavier mining machinery out from Dawson.

Of the Dawson-to-Grand Forks freighters, Orr & Tukey was one of the largest, most reliable and longest tenured. The company ran at least one round-trip stage between Dawson and Grand Forks every day of the week for years.

The stage left Dawson at 8 A.M., arriving in Grand Forks at about noon—traveling an average of three and a half miles per hour—depending on the size and weight of the load. The return trip, which left the Forks at 3 P.M. and arrived in Dawson at 7:30 P.M., was a little slower because of the uphill grade.

Orr & Tukey carried an average of four to eight tons of freight per run and charged $12 a ton; just a few years earlier packers had received up to 20 cents a pound when gold was first discovered and there was no Ridge Road. More important, Orr & Tukey carried mail—on an informal basis until 1900, and then under contract with the territorial government until 1903, when the firm refused to continue after not being paid for those three years!

Orr & Tukey was awarded the mail contract as the low bidder, charging the government $30 for weekly mail runs from Dawson to the Forks

This North American Transportation & Trading Company sleigh was used for winter deliveries along the creeks.

and on to Hunker Creek. Additional runs were added at $10 each. Weekly mail delivery to Last Chance was $60, to Sulphur was $40 and to Dominion and Gold Run was $80 each. Even when conditions were so bad that freight runs had to be postponed, an Orr & Tukey rider or driver still carried the mail. During the long winter, that mail was one of the most welcome sights to miners.

It wasn't really a glacier, but the countryside was still white outside of Grand Forks in June when this stage took a break along the Ridge Road between Dawson and Grand Forks.

When the rush was at its peak, there were several freighters, but most were one-man, one-wagon operations, with the owners out to earn a quick buck. As the Klondike population stabilized, so did the list of permanent freighters. In addition to Orr & Tukey, Charles Bell, L.C. Lane, Robertson & Company, Door and Wright, the Reeves Stage Line, and H.H. Honnen Company, one of the earliest, were at the Forks. Honnen soon sold his company and used the profits to open a mining company, which eventually evolved into the Violet Mining Group, a conglomerate with interests in several parts of the district. The new owners of Honnen's company called the firm the Dawson Transfer Company and operated three stages daily out of Dawson, leaving at 9 A.M. and 6 P.M. for Bonanza and at 5 P.M. for Hunker and Gold Bottom. Going the other way, stages left Bonanza at 8 A.M. and 6 P.M. and Gold Bottom at 8 A.M. One-way Bonanza-to-Dawson fare was $2, and a round-trip ticket cost $3.50.

First Avenue in Grand Forks. Mary Kinsey is in the white blouse and Clarence is in the striped shirt, vest and dark hat. These buildings were just down from the Orr & Tukey office. Dawson Transfer Company was the successor of an early Klondike freighter, H.H. Honnen, who sold out and formed the Violet Mining Group, which owned four claims and one fraction on Eldorado.

Next to the Dawson Stage Line was a barber shop, then Johnston & Safford's general mercantile (in the process of holding a going-out-of-business sale), a newsstand and Christie & Hadley's general store. Hadley and another Bonanza merchant, a Mr. Short, owned the Colorado Roadhouse at Carmack's Forks.

ALL NIGHT
RESTAURANT.
DAWSON TRANSFER CO.
STAGE LINE TO
DAWSON,
SUCCESSORS TO H.H. HONNEN.
GOING OUT OF BUSINESS.
EVERY THING AT COST.
CHRISTIE & HADLEY
MERCHANDISE

A.M.D.GLADWIN, PROP.

Roadhouses

Many of the freight companies also carried passengers and freight along the other main highway of the Yukon—the road that stretched 320 miles south to Whitehorse. The trip took five and a half days, with stops at least every twenty miles for a change of horses.

Small pockets of civilization cropped up at these stopping points, out along the creeks and along the road to Whitehorse. There was at least one roadhouse at every twenty-mile interval, but often several were clustered together in the same general area.

Orr & Tukey had one advantage over the competition; it served as an agent for the White Pass & Yukon Route, which also operated its own horse-drawn coaches and sleighs in the Yukon. A typical overland fare from Dawson to Whitehorse was $150 per person while the gold rush demand was at its peak, but that dropped to $100 and less once the feverish pace subsided.

In addition to passengers, one of the main things carried into the Klondike was something in great demand with miners—eggs. In summer eggs could be hauled easily from Whitehorse by stage, but in winter the cold weather was a problem. So freighters hired Grand Forks and Dawson schoolboys as candlers—they sat in the back of the wagon keeping candles lit to prevent

This was one of the less elaborate of the dozens of way stations along the creeks, but it offered the necessities—a place to sleep, freight service and hot meals.

The McDonald Hotel lacked the comforts of large Dawson hotels, but it was warm and dry, thanks in part to the chinking between the logs of the building. The McDonald even had glass in the windows AND curtains.

the eggs from freezing. The candling was important, since frozen eggs were just about worthless—although not quite; they always brought a few cents as a supplement for dog food. Summer egg prices dipped to a dollar a dozen, but in winter the price rose to as much as $4.50.

Whitehorse stages made meal stops twice daily, while the horse teams were changed, overnighting at roadhouses at the end of each roughly 60-mile day. Henry G. "Hank" West opened the first roadhouse—the Flag—beyond the Forks in 1898, paving the way for the dozens of others that followed.

Along the claims the less-elegant facilities were housed in large tents or one-story cabins, but several of the better roadhouses were well-constructed two-story buildings. Some were nearly as fancy as Grand Forks or Dawson hotels, in many cases offering guests much more than a night's lodging. Virtually all had good restaurants and well-stocked stores with liquor, tobacco, miscellaneous supplies and bulk food.

The list of well-furnished roadhouses included the Colorado at Carmack's Forks (owned by Grand Forks merchants Hadley and Short); West's Number 17 Below on Dominion; John J. McPhee's Whitehouse on Number 26 Eldorado; Williams' Roadhouse (sold in 1900 to brothers George A. and W.A. Murray) at the junction of Gold Run and Dominion Roads; Number 96 Above on Bonanza, owned by L.J. McCarty and his wife; and a string of stops owned by Mrs. J. Carroll, whose long list included Number 57 Below on Bonanza, Number 30 Gold Run, the Dome Roadhouse, an unnamed building at the mouth of Eureka Creek and even a hotel at Nome during the rush there.

Perhaps the nicest roadhouse of all was the Gold Run Hotel. The $25,000 two-story structure had white enameled bedsteads with brass trimmings, central heating, an adjacent bathhouse and even asbestos wall insulation for fireproofing. The Gold Run also provided accommodations for many of the 150 men employed in the nearby mining properties.

Many of the way stations had bars, and more than a few offered guests gambling and prostitutes. But the government's attitude toward both was much less lenient than in the towns. In fact, soon after the Canadian government realized that the population inside the Klondike was permanent, officials decided that some things had to be changed in the roadhouses since they often were an Outsider's first introduction to the Klondike.

The Murray brothers' roadhouse was one of the best. It was on Number 33 Below on Lower Dominion, 37 miles from Dawson. It had a pay phone, 25-cent beer and excellent accommodations. Agnes Kinsey operated the roadhouse for the owner when one of the Murrays became ill. Olive Kinsey and her dog, Dick, are on the porch.

MURRAY'S HOTEL.
33 Below Lower
TELEPHONE Pay Station
37
McLENNAN'S DRY GOODS STORE

An Orr & Tukey stage making a freight stop at Joe Nee's roadhouse. The roadhouse offered beds, food and drink—and perhaps a bit more—around the clock. Nee ran afoul of the law for allowing "known dance hall girls" on the premises and for allowing them to serve drinks.

Legislated Morality

In 1901 a general edict was issued to clean up the Klondike and to regulate prostitution and gambling not only from Dawson to Grand Forks, but from roadhouses throughout the territory.

Prostitutes, who often used cigar stores or dressmakers' shops as fronts, were allowed to remain in Grand Forks but were strictly forbidden from selling their wares anywhere but along their row of cabins. The prostitutes of Dawson were treated more harshly. The 50 or so still in town were ordered to vacate their downtown cabins along Fourth and Fifth avenues and were allowed to work only across the Klondike River in the community known as Klondike City or Lousetown.

Gambling was outlawed altogether, putting about 300 Klondikers out of work, and liquor and dance hall regulations were tightened considerably. Officials even went so far as to pay two undercover agents $6 each per day to spend a month visiting dance halls and hotels to collect evidence against "women of loose moral character."

New ordinances made it illegal to serve women drinks in dance halls, for women to serve liquor in any public place, for gold to be used as payment in bars or for males under 21 to work or to be served in a place where liquor was served. And a conviction on any violation resulted in the offender being barred from employment in the industry anywhere in the Klondike. The laws were strict, but the police were very deliberate. They refused to press charges against anyone unless there was overwhelming evidence that would ensure a conviction.

When local ministers and visiting members of the Women's Christian Temperance Union from the East, among others, filed vague charges based on what the Mounted Police determined to be no more than hearsay, local merchants were quick to react. A petition carrying several pages of signatures from leading businessmen and women was presented to the government, adamantly asking that the few remaining dance halls not be closed; they were still the main drawing card that brought miners into town.

Horses were used on the claims to haul timber or pull plows. The power plant (with the large stack) on this claim indicated the change from slow bonfire thawing to the steam era. But despite this early mechanization, men with shovels were still the mainstay of Klondike mining.

—IV—

The Last Good Years

The peak years for the Klondike and for Grand Forks were so brief that they were over before they could be enjoyed. Almost simultaneously the gold rush disappeared, the new century arrived and the pace slowed.

In terms of gold production, 1900 was the biggest year in the Klondike; in terms of government services and social progress, 1901 and 1902 were the best years for those living in Grand Forks. But the progress came too late. In 1901 Raymond Jullien had all the rooms wired at the Northern—the first hotel at Grand Forks to offer electricity in its guest rooms. That same year the Kinseys were finally able to afford their two-story wood-frame studio in downtown Grand Forks, but it wasn't completed until 1902, when the government reevaluated the town and lowered all the property values. Just as Clarke and Clarence Kinsey and many others at the Forks started to prosper, the decline began.

The power plants at Tom Lippy's claim ran both the steam pipes and electric lights. The crews worked about 17 feet below the creek level in cavernous pits that sometimes were as much as several hundred feet wide or long. Steam from the pipes melted the dirt so the pick and shovel crews could dig out the dirt and put it into buckets. The diggings were hoisted up, then shoveled into the sluices for washing out.

Dance halls and saloons were closing as the federal government doled out money to fund schools, fire and police protection and other services. By "civilizing" the Klondike, the government was inadvertently hastening the end.

Gold production, which dictated directly and indirectly everything that happened in the Klondike, told the story explicitly. During the first year of the rush, in 1897, miners took out an estimated $2.5 million in gold. The figure jumped to $10 million in 1898, $16 million in 1899 and to $22 million in 1900. But that was the top. The figures dropped from there, year after year—$18 million in 1901, $14.5 million in 1902, $12.3 million in 1903 and only $9.4 million in 1904.

In a move that temporarily spurred the economy in 1901, the government opened several of its claims for staking on Eldorado Creek. The snow was waist-deep the night hundreds of miners crowded in doorways waiting for 12:01—when the stream was officially opened. Each miner harbored visions of finally making the big discovery that so far had been elusive. But as had happened so often before, there were no grand results—at least not

KLONDIKE GOLD PRODUCTION

Year	Gold— Millions of Dollars
1885-1896	$ 2.0
1897	2.5
1898	10.0
1899	16.0
1900	22.3
1901	18.0
1902	14.5
1903	12.3
1904	9.4
1905	7.2
1906	5.3
1907	2.9
1908	3.3
1909	4.0
1910	4.6
1911	4.6
1912	5.0
*Other, through 1912	25.9
Total, 1885-1912	**$175 million**

*This includes gold produced near the Klondike (such as at Forty Mile and Eagle, Alaska) and shipped through Dawson, plus small amounts the Canadian government estimates were produced in the Klondike but never taxed.

The town of Grand Forks at its most metropolitan: First Avenue ran from the NAT&T store, parallel to Bonanza Creek (in the foreground), past the various hotels. The other main street was Second Avenue, which was lined with cabins and ran roughly parallel to First. Second turned until it intersected First at about a 45-degree angle (near the left of the photo). Eldorado Road ran off to the right and Bonanza Road to the left, both out of the picture.

DRUGGIST

Elaborate tramways were eventually built to carry diggings off hillsides. This Gold Hill claim was worked all winter. Diggings were brought down the hillside on rail cars on the elevated track and the huge pile at the bottom was worked through the sluices when the spring thaw came.

Klondike mining was more mechanized than most Outsiders thought, even in the first few years. Numbers 14, 15 and 16 Below Discovery on Bonanza belonged to David McKay, Harry Waugh, Dan McGilvary and Dave Edwards. They had staked the second claim downstream from Carmack's discovery on Bonanza, but found little gold and quickly sold out for $15,000, moving downstream—where they found a rich paystreak and operated a thirty-five-man crew year-round.

at first. Then, just before spring breakup, a new streak of gold was unearthed. It ran almost 100 feet deep, more than twice as deep as the original seam of gold that had made so many men wealthy earlier.

There were no new millionaires, but Grand

Spring cleanup was the culmination of months of hard work. The gold in the sluices was the reason. Riffles or slats would catch the gold as it progressed toward the end of the box. The slats got continually smaller to catch the finer bits of gold, with a piece of rug or canvas at the end catching most of the smaller particles. Quicksilver was often used as a last step to recover the smallest bits of dust. The whisk broom was used in the final step and this was the work no one seemed to mind—sweeping the gold out of the sluice boxes.

Forks enjoyed a last bit of glory. The entire Klondike had a population of only 27,219 by then, with just over 9,000 in Dawson and even fewer at the Forks and along the streams. The once-burgeoning population was beginning to decline.

One segment of the population was growing unchecked, however. Dogs, once worth hundreds of dollars, were roaming the streets of Grand Forks and Dawson. Rabid animals were shot on the streets on several occasions and abandoned animals scavanged the city streets for food. A $2 license fee was instituted, but it had little effect. Anyone interested in his or her animals took care of them; those who didn't care simply let their dogs fend for themselves, ignoring the new law.

Shelters built in both towns soon contained dozens of animals.

Clarke and Mary Kinsey did their best to help in more than one way. In 1900 they adopted Dick, a shaggy black Newfoundland pup, and on Dominion Day 1902 their second son Ronald increased the population by one. The Kinseys all lived on Gold Hill, but Clarke and Clarence also built an apartment in the new studio building across from Walter Woodburn's drug store on First Avenue. The apartment was soon put to good use. In 1903 Clarence married Agnes Fisher and the couple set up housekeeping in back of the studio on the second floor. The first floor was leased to the Grand Forks Commission House, a general merchant.

The Forks no longer had the look of a boom town. It was lined with telephone poles and dotted with several modern, two-story buildings and as many wood-frame stores as log cabins.

The Mechanized Years, The Declining Years

The beginning of the end in the Klondike took place in the gold fields, and followed almost immediately the brief glory and temporary growth spurred by the 1901 strike on Eldorado Creek. That year the first gold dredge began operating in the Klondike. Although no more than a novelty to most of those who watched it, the dredge signaled the end of one of the most glorious periods in North American history. Twentieth-century mechanization was the single overriding factor that buried the Klondike society—literally and figuratively.

This mechanization was far different from the earlier gradual changes to steam points, self-dumping buckets and electrically powered generators. Gold production had declined despite those improvements. The only way to extract the shrinking supply of gold from the

Dredges, more than any other single thing, were the deathblow to the Klondike gold era. The supply of gold was dwindling, so more land had to be moved to find it, and the dredges were far more economical than crews of miners working the land.

Klondike and still make money now was by spending big money, which meant big companies and their big dredges.

Clarke and Clarence enjoyed their most prosperous years as the changes occurred. From 1902 to 1904 they operated their photography business out of their new downtown studio, but Clarence also supervised a crew of several men on their Gold Hill claim. Clarence and Agnes's first child, Olive, was born in 1904.

Several members of both the Kinsey and Fisher families went North to visit, work and enjoy the last fleeting bit of the Klondike gold era. Louisa Kinsey and her sons Edmund and Alfred were caught up in the magic of the North. Agnes's brother Bob had gone to the Klondike in 1898 from Newfoundland, later bringing Agnes and their sister Virtue to Grand Forks.

Clarke's propensity for people and cameras, and Clarence's equally strong ambition to mine, became more obvious. Their partnership flourished. Clarke spent the majority of his time with his camera, snapping pictures of parties and people, often setting the camera for a delayed exposure so he could run to the other side and join his friends in the photograph. Clarence, too, enjoyed the parties, but spent more time with a shovel than with a camera in his hands.

There were still parties on Dominion Day and Independence Day, with some of the events as glorious during this period as earlier. Everyone was even more patient with life than they had been a few years before. Those who lived in Grand Forks were there because it was their home. The pace was slow and the society was as close-knit as ever, and that was one of the factors that kept so many people in Grand Forks after the gold began to disappear.

The buildings and homes that were being used in Grand Forks were more modern than any had been before, but no new buildings were built and people were leaving by the dozens—by the hundreds. Those who remained, however, seemed oblivious to the change.

A single dance hall remained in Grand Forks, and only two were left in Dawson. Even the entertainment was different: now there were vaudeville and stage shows, motion pictures and boxing exhibitions. There was little illicit activity for the government to control. Only a total of about two dozen prostitutes remained in Dawson and Grand Forks, and the territorial court tried as many cases in an entire year as it had in a single month just a few years earlier. One by one government offices closed at the Forks, and stores sold out their entire stocks as the owners salvaged what they could from their investments and left.

As the population dwindled, 29-year-old Clarke became uneasy; he had stayed because of the people. He enjoyed commercial photography, but he could enjoy it more and prosper more from it Outside. The people had kept him in Grand Forks, so when they left his decision to leave was relatively easy. The Kinsey & Kinsey partnership was dissolved. In 1906, Clarke,

The Anderson Concession on Hunker Creek illustrated the changes that took place over the years in the Klondike. This was once a thriving mine but as the production began to slow, shafts and sluices were replaced by dredges. The Yukon Gold Company built its Dredge Number 4 on this site in 1908, working the claim until 1910.

In 1902 the Kinsey studio was completed in downtown Grand Forks. At the back of the studio was an elegant and comfortable apartment (left), where Clarence, Agnes and Olive lived for several years. The skylight, unusual in 1902, was built to provide daylight for studio work. Clarke is on the stairs (wearing the bow tie); Clarence is directly behind him.

Previous page: A panorama of Tom Lippy's claim where he and his crew mined over $1 million in gold. Number 16 Eldorado was dotted with stacks from power plants and shafts, as well as crisscrossed with sluiceways. There were several cabins on the claim for the owner, crew and for storage. The Ridge Road from Grand Forks to Dawson led out of town through the valley between the hills in the background. Downtown Grand Forks was out of the picture to the left.
J.J. Putraw managed the Lippy claim whenever Lippy was away, which was often. James Goff and Ed Crawford were the foremen. About 40 men worked on the claim in the fall and winter, but that figure swelled to 200 in the spring and summer—the largest crew on any single claim in the Klondike. Laborers earned the going rate of $1 per hour. Once the washing out began, the yield was about $6,000 a day.

Mary and their two boys left for Seattle. They took what furniture was practical to pack and several hundred glass-plate negatives.

The heavy, six-and-a-half- by eight-and-a-half-inch and eleven- by fourteen-inch negatives were Clarke's personal scrapbook of nearly eight years of his life, eight years that saw Grand Forks grow and prosper, then fade as quickly as the gold did.

Clarence's decision was even easier than Clarke's. The glass plates still read Kinsey & Kinsey, but Clarence's new partner was Agnes and besides, photography was little more than a hobby for them. Clarence continued to operate the mine, and he and Agnes settled into a more isolated lifestyle. Clarence, always quieter than his younger brother, enjoyed mining far more than even he had realized. He wasn't a miner like most of the thousands who had come before him searching for wealth; he was there because he enjoyed the looking, and had he ever struck it rich he probably still would have continued mining, looking for new veins of gold.

By 1906, when Clarke left, there were four dredges operating in the Klondike, and the mining inspector's office just down the street on First Avenue was boarded up and vacant. What once were stream banks lined by miners and their cabins and sluices became endless fields of symmetrical mounds of dredged-through waste.

There were still several thousand people living in Dawson, and as many working out along the streams. But most were working for the big eastern corporations that were taking what gold was left. Those who weren't mining were operating the stores and hotels.

That same year one of the most novel ideas, one that had first been discussed as far back as 1898, became a reality: a railroad was built. It had been in many people's minds when they saw how successful the White Pass & Yukon Route had been and how much it had done for the gold rush and the Klondike. But no one went so far as to attempt construction until 1903.

Grading work had begun along Bonanza Creek in 1903, and between three and four miles of track were laid before the project was abandoned for lack of funding and workable plans. Work was revived in 1906, with better financial backing and a comprehensive plan. A new right of way was graded from Dawson to the Forks and beyond to Sulphur Springs, a total of thirty-two miles. By November of that year the line was operational.

The new Klondike Mines Railway replaced the White Pass line as the farthest north on the continent. Local contractors, first Jerome Chute (during the ill-fated 1903 attempt) and then the firm of O'Brien and Mackenzie, built the line. A civil engineer, J.W. Astley, was the first manager and chief engineer. The railroad was

A Klondike Mines Railway train pulling out of downtown Dawson, heading for Grand Forks.
(Courtesy of the University of Alaska Library)

Not Good if Detached

KLONDIKE MINES RY. CO.
Good for one continuous passage
FROM
GRAND FORKS, Y. T.
TO
DAWSON, Y. T.
If presented on date stamped on back.
H. D Weeks, Gen. Agt.
No. D..........

KLONDIKE MINES RY. CO.
Good for one continuous passage
FROM
DAWSON, Y. T.
TO
GRAND FORKS, Y. T.
If presented within 15 days from date stamped on back.
H. D. Weeks, Gen. Agt.
No. D..........

The railroad was a boon to Klondike freight shippers, but like so many of the era's mechanizations, its success was short-lived.
(Courtesy of Mrs. Malcolm MacMillan)

One of the early boiler-equipped claims, this hillside mine was somewhat unusual in that it was worked with a tunnel rather a shaft.

put into service as soon as it was completed, but that was the only winter the line ever ran—or tried to. The weather conditions were too severe. But in the spring of 1907, the locomotives were steaming out of downtown Dawson, heading for the creeks and loaded with passengers and freight.

Another equally ambitious project was started during the same period. A steel pipeline was built stretching 75 miles through the gold fields to carry water for hydraulic mining. With the steel rails, dredge components and the massive steel pipeline sections, freighters in the area were coping with an entirely new set of hauling requirements. It was slow and difficult to haul pipe or rail to the creeks by horse and wagon team. Two or three dredge buckets were an entire wagonload. And once the railroad was completed, horse-drawn wagons went back to hauling lighter freight.

The new gold dredges kept the Klondike alive, sifting dirt, gravel and gold for only a few cents a cubic yard. Eventually more than a dozen of the machines worked up and down the creeks.

Beginning in 1906 the Yukon Gold Company operated several dredges, including Numbers 1 and 2 on Lower Bonanza. The machines eventually took a total of $6 million in gold out of the creek, but it took fourteen years to do it. A third dredge worked Lower Bonanza and Bear Creek, producing $2.5 million in gold. Each of the three machines was nearly twice the size of the first Klondike dredge.

A total of six more Yukon Gold dredges, all with seven-cubic-yard buckets, worked up and down Bonanza, Gold Run, Dominion and Eldorado creeks, going through Tom Lippy's

Hydraulic mining was common in the later years of the gold era, with large steel pipes and nozzles doing the work that men had done earlier with plows, picks and shovels. The pressure of the water could rip off not only the top layer of moss and soil, but loose rock and gravel, as well.

Overleaf: Hydraulic mining was a mainstay of Klondike mining by 1904, when this photo was taken. Powerful streams of water were used to move the gravel down the hillside, where it could be washed out to recover the gold.

INSEY&KINSEY PHOTO.
11 BELOW DISCOVERY BONANZA.

Claim Number 16. All told, the six machines dredged up $16.6 million in gold in roughly a decade, while from 1897 to 1904 the same streams had yielded $100 million.

The Lewes River Mining and Dredging Company, which had started it all with the first dredge in 1901, continued to operate that single machine until 1908.

The other dredging operation, the Canadian Klondyke Mining Company, Ltd., had one seven-yard model and the three giants of the mining district: Dredge Number 2 with fifteen-yard buckets and Numbers 3 and 4 with sixteen-yard buckets.

Those largest dredges, then the biggest in the world, had 68-foot-wide decks and housings built over 56- by 136-foot frames. Each machine had a 68-bucket chain, with each bucket weighing some 4,700 pounds. A 10- by 50-foot screen sifted the gold from the dirt and gravel. Each machine, built at a cost of about $500,000, weighed almost four and a half million pounds.

Klondyke Mining eventually sold out to a new company, the Yukon Consolidated Gold Company, but before the industry was dead in the Klondike, those four dredges took nearly $27 million more out of the ground.

While the dredges worked, the Klondike society lost whatever stability remained, and the population continued to decline. The people who had given the Klondike its color, after sharing in its glory, drifted away.

This photo was taken at about the time the dredges began to move in. Steam billowed from a power plant and wood was stockpiled for firing the boilers and for use in the sluices. Wood for the sluices was either whipsawed or machine sawed on the site.

Belinda sold her mining interests, continuing to make her business deals at the most profitable times. After selling her hotel in Dawson, which represented a very small part of her financial empire, she and the count spent summers in France, and at one time Belinda had more than $1 million in gold in her Paris bank account.

She went to Fairbanks after the gold rush there, making several investments and serving as one of the principals of the Dome Bank in the nearby community of the same name.

Yukon Gold Company's dredge Number 8 under construction at Grand Forks in 1911; note the difference in the downtown compared to earlier years.

(Public Archives of Canada, courtesy of Lewis Green)

Clarke took his favorite glass-plate negatives Outside with him. This one, which didn't survive the trip in one piece, shows Clarke's wife Mary seated at the right and Clarence's wife Agnes at her right. Agnes, her sister Virtue, and her brother Bob had been at the Forks two years when Clarence and Agnes married.

Belinda often traveled to Seattle, as she had been doing since her first years in the North. After leaving Dome when the bank was closed in 1910, she spent only a little more time in Alaska before settling permanently Outside. On one of her last trips Outside before moving south, one final incident took place that epitomized her independent nature.

In 1911, while Belinda and her sister Margaret were staying at the Washington Hotel in downtown Seattle, an Alaskan, A.F. Ruser, began making boisterous accusations about their wrongdoing at Dome.

Belinda and the slightly less outgoing Margaret remained quiet until Ruser accused Margaret of embezzling funds from the bank while she was working as a teller there. Belinda angrily confronted Ruser in the hotel lobby, grabbed a horsewhip and in front of a lobby full of friends and strangers, began whipping Ruser until he cried and begged her to stop.

Even after this incident Ruser refused to keep quiet, and told everyone that Belinda had had help in beating him. He then went one step further and asked the local prosecutor to issue a warrant for Belinda's arrest for assaulting him. But the local authorities ignored him, apparently agreeing with Belinda's allegation that "a blackmailer simply received a little Alaska justice."

Shortly afterward, Belinda invested a small bit of her fortune in an elegant home known as the Castle, which she had built in the eastern Washington community of Yakima.

That was Belinda's last bit of fame and flamboyance. The Carbonneaus then invested her entire fortune in a steamship company, an apparently sound investment. Some reports list

A family portrait taken by Clarke of his wife Mary (standing) and their first son Leonard, with Clarence and his wife Agnes.

the breakout of World War I as the reason for the subsequent bankruptcy of the company, although that is only speculation. For whatever reason, the Carbonneaus lost the fortune Belinda had earned in the Klondike.

Belinda had little money left, her multi-million-dollar list of investments wiped out by a single bit of bad luck, bad investment or perhaps dishonesty.

The war brought another loss; Charles went to France and an account of his death on the battlefront was widely circulated; he reportedly was killed by shrapnel while serving as a purchasing agent for the French government. But a little mystery remained.

A short news item in the Dawson newspaper at the end of the war mentioned the death of Charles Eugene Carbonneau, described as a well-known Klondiker of a decade earlier. In the unverified report, the paper said that Carbonneau had died in France, but in prison after going insane following his arrest. He reportedly had been apprehended in South America after absconding with a million dollars.

Belinda, no longer surrounded by the colorful characters of her youth, lived a quiet life that lasted for nearly half a century more.

She stayed at the Castle for years, finally moving to a Seattle nursing home when the combination of her years and the size of her large Yakima home became too much for her. She died in 1967 at 95, rich with memories tempered a bit by the years, and without a penny of the millions she had earned in the Klondike.

A "modern" Klondike home, shown in the latter years of the gold era (1912); it was far more comfortable than most Klondike cabins of just a few years earlier.

Few who had approached Belinda's wealth enjoyed her happiness or longevity. Big Alex McDonald, one of the wealthiest miners, suffered a heart attack while chopping wood at his cabin and died while the Klondike rush was still at its peak. Dick Lowe, once a millionaire, from his famous fraction, spent it all plus a little more and died penniless and an alcoholic in 1907. Antone Stander's young bride eventually spent all of his money and ruined him, too.

Robert Henderson, the acknowledged "co-discoverer" of that wealth of gold, died bitter, still searching for the Klondike mother lode. Tom Lippy was a partial exception, living a long life; but in his naivete he squandered his wealth on poor investments. He died owing a fortune instead of having one. George Carmack, however, was one exception. His fortune took him on a round-the-world yacht trip and he died a wealthy man.

Clarence Berry, and his brother and sometimes partner Frank, continued their good fortune after the Klondike dried up. They followed the gold to Fairbanks where their good luck continued, and eventually they returned to California where they parlayed their yellow gold into a fortune in black gold, as well.

The Kinseys, never obsessed with the gold that had brought them to Grand Forks, were never destroyed by it.

Clarke, who had returned to Seattle in 1906, operated a construction company until about 1913, keeping only peripherally involved in photography. But he soon found that he was a far better photographer than construction man. He returned to commercial photography and spent half a century working up and down the West Coast. Clarke and Darius earned local and national recognition for their excellent photography of the timber industry, which far out-stripped Clarke and Clarence's Klondike work, at least in terms of technical quality.

Clarence remained in Grand Forks for a few years after Clarke left, while there still was a town to live in. In 1908, he, Agnes and Olive moved out to Dominion Creek, where he continued to mine. Alfred Kinsey and his wife Lila joined them that year, and the two couples filed claims in the names of the four and worked them together. The Lizzie Mineral Claim officially belonged to Alfred, the New York to Lila, the Daisy to Clarence and the Short Cut Number 2 to Agnes.

But in 1911 Agnes became seriously ill and had no choice but to leave the North. She and Olive moved to Seattle, while Clarence remained in the Klondike working the family claims. But Agnes was more ill than they thought, so Clarence joined her, staying with Darius and his wife Tabitha while Agnes was hospitalized. The short stay turned into weeks and then months. Finally, after nearly a year, Agnes regained her health and the family was off again. They had never gotten the Klondike out of their blood and decided to return.

Clarence and Agnes spent some time in Dawson, in Mayo and out along Haggart Creek. Among their mines were the Clara Claim on Dominion, the Olive Mineral Claim (named for their daughter) and the Exchange Mineral Claim, which had originally belonged to Agnes's brother Bob.

None of Clarence's claims were big producers. Still, mining was a way of life that he hated to give up. Finally, in 1919, he moved back Outside and went to work in a veterans' home at Retsil, Washington (just west of Seattle near Bremerton), and never again went back to mining or photography. He worked at the veterans' home for almost thirty years, retiring in 1949, seven years before he died at the age of 84 in 1956.

A few months after Clarence's death, Clarke, the last of the children Edmund and Louisa Kinsey had brought to Snoqualmie in 1890, died at 79. More than the passing of all those who lived the Klondike gold era was the saddest death of all—the death of the Klondike itself.

The boom town of Grand Forks really died when the gold dredges moved in, but it was a slow death. The North West Mounted Police phased out the Bonanza Detachment as the population dwindled, and in 1909 only one Mounty remained. Then, as the dredges moved closer and closer to town while working their way along Bonanza Creek, the ground became unstable. The police buildings were put up for sale and the one-man Grand Forks detachment moved into a small cabin on safer ground; the rent on the cabin was less than the heating bill for the two-story headquarters building.

The Yukon Gold Company agreed to buy the police buildings for storage, but a fire broke out

After Clarke left, Clarence continued to mine in the Klondike. This claim, just one of those he worked, was named for his daughter Olive. Although the photo looks as if it predates the gold era, it was taken in 1912 and typifies the "old west" style of mining envisioned by people Outside. Bob Fisher is third from left, sitting above the mine entrance.

OLIVE
MINERAL
CLAIM
DUBLIN
GULCH
Y.T.

and destroyed the wooden structures before anything was moved in. There were fewer than 10,000 people in the entire territory by then, about a third of them in Dawson and less than a third working for the dredging companies.

The Grand Forks constable had little to do; by 1911 he had been transferred. What was left of Grand Forks was without one more of its shrinking list of public servants.

The Gold Hill school remained, but just barely. The enrollment was nine, enough to continue receiving funding as an assisted school. Gold Bottom, the largest assisted school in the territory, had an enrollment of eleven. Still, officials of the territory held out hopes that the schools would experience a growth in enrollment, looking to wives and children to join the dredge workers in the area. But it never happened.

The Grand Forks school was a shambles. Mrs. Clark, the teacher, received $100 a month—$50 less than her predecessors—and complained vehemently to the territorial government about the conditions. She had been forced to make repairs to the building herself as well as serving as a janitor after the government's funding cutback. Most of the textbooks were in bad shape, and the school was without a single atlas or dictionary since those had been loaned to the Gold Bottom school and never returned or replaced.

Mrs. Clark, who was paid only for the months when she taught, petitioned for a $25-a-month raise, out of which she offered to hire a carpenter to repair the building and a janitor to clean it regularly. Despite the government's statement that it hoped for an increase in enrollment, it refused her request for more money.

Churches and stores were abandoned and demolished, the Klondike Mines Railway quit operating and the old dance halls were no more than a memory. People continued to leave the Yukon, Dawson and what was left of Grand Forks.

Then, in 1921, some of the world's largest dredges, which continued to chew up the Klondike until the 1960's, moved along Bonanza Creek and through Grand Forks. Meanwhile, hydraulic mining stripped off much of Gold Hill, and the tailings were dumped on what once had been the thriving town of Grand Forks.

A modern Yukon home, long after Clarke had left, at Highet Creek, one of the many places where Clarence mined.

Klondike Lost

Today, less than 1,000 people still call Dawson City home, but the territorial government moved from there to Whitehorse in 1953. Tourism has kept Dawson alive since then, but often just barely.

The Canadian government recently began a long-term program to restore the Klondike—the gold rush buildings in Dawson and some of the areas out along the creeks. However, there are no definite plans for Grand Forks. A sign marks the spot where part of the town once existed, and an enlargement of a photograph Clarke and Clarence took just after the turn of the century gives visitors a vague idea of what once existed there.

Bonanza Creek winds along roughly the same path it always did, through the valley until it joins the Klondike River near Dawson. Two cabins are perched rather precariously above the creek, and the overgrown remains of the cemetery are still visible beyond the former townsite.

On Gold Hill, hidden in 75 years' growth of trees and moss, is a pile of boards—remains of what was once the school; another crumple of boards at the place where one of the community's churches once stood, bears a resemblance to a steeple; and there are a couple of well-built cabins defying the years and an equally well-constructed outhouse still standing.

Scattered along the spongy hillside are rusted heaps of cans, garbage piles from the last miners who lived there. Behind the site of the school, in the cabin where Miss Keyes and then Mrs. Clark

One of the cabins in what was once the town of Grand Forks. Remarkably well built, the logs on this wall (facing downstream toward Dawson) look as though they could have been cut just a few years ago. Bits of sod and canvas—used to seal and insulate the walls—hang from the logs. Inside, the wood still looks fresh, showing no signs of rotting; the wall looks sturdy enough to last another 80 years. (Norm Bolotin)

Right—What's left of Grand Forks furniture—an old cupboard that probably was pulled from a cabin by souvenir hunters. The shelves are still intact, and tattered pieces of decorative paper still hang from the sides.

(Norm Bolotin)

Far right: Another of the few buildings still standing at Grand Forks—an old but very well-built outhouse, on Gold Hill. Surrounding the clump of remaining buildings are piles of hundreds of rusted cans, homemade utensils (such as a lantern made from a syrup can), moldy footwear and other overgrown relics.

(Norm Bolotin)

This is all that remains of the Gold Hill school at Grand Forks. A miner who has worked in the area since the late 1920's said that old school books, bits of paper and benches were in this heap until a few years ago, when souvenir hunters began taking away everything they could carry.

(Norm Bolotin)

Grand Forks today. The little trickle of water is Bonanza Creek. This photograph was taken looking toward Dawson, from near the spot where Coutts Stable once stood. (Norm Bolotin)

probably lived, a few crude pieces of furniture lie exposed to the weather. An old wood-and-wire cot is half covered with leaves outside the other cabin.

Canadian law now makes it illegal to disturb historic sites, but over the years souvenir hunters have picked up bits and pieces of Klondike history that littered the landscape. Some have even gone so far as to tear boards off the few remaining Grand Forks cabins when they needed firewood.

Today, staring up and down the little trickle of water known as Bonanza Creek, it is difficult to imagine that 10,000 men, women and children once made the area their home. Only a handful of those people are still alive today, and in a few years they will be gone, too.

For years the Kinsey legacy was thought to be the thousands of timber-industry photographs that Clarke and Darius had taken over a combined total of nearly 100 years of work. But, because somewhere a few old prints survived, and because Clarke decided to take his personal collection of glass-plate negatives to Seattle with him in 1906, there still is a Grand Forks.

It would have been a shame to have buried such a glorious town without even a headstone to mark the grave. Fortunately, Clarke and Clarence left a vivid epitaph in their photos, attesting to what a truly remarkable town Grand Forks once was.

Clarence Kinsey, seen here loading luggage in a wagon at the foot of the stairs to the Kinseys' studio, stayed at the Forks long after most residents had left. And he spent several years more mining throughout the Yukon before finally giving up and heading back to the Seattle area.

Death Closes Chapter in Valley History

The death on Nov. 29 [1956] of Clarke Kinsey closed a chapter in the history of the Snoqualmie Valley, for Mr. Kinsey was the last surviving member of a family which moved to Snoqualmie in 1890. He was preceded in death earlier this year by a brother, Clarence Kinsey who died in March, and by a sister, Mrs. Emily Odell, who passed away on Sept. 8.

Clarke Kinsey, 79, died at his home in Seattle after having been in failing health for months. Funeral services were held in the Home Undertaking Co. chapel on Saturday, Dec. 1.

Survivors include his wife, Minnie M.; a son, Ronald C. Kinsey, Washington D.C., three daughters, Mrs. Harlan Cavender and Mrs. Leonard Mannon, both of Seattle, and Mrs. Byron R. Davis, Olympia. Also seven grandchildren, one great-grandchild and two nieces Mrs. Joe Seil and Mrs. Bill Carey, both of Snoqualmie.

Mr. Kinsey, who was born in Maryville, Mo., came to the Valley with his parents, the late Mr. and Mrs. Edmond Kinsey. His mother missed by only 48 hours being the first woman in Snoqualmie; she arrived just a couple of days after Mrs. Klaus, who assisted her husband in the operation of a shoe shop. Kinsey's brothers, Darius and Alfred, came ahead of the rest of the family and were on the very first train that ever pulled into town.

Another first established by the Kinseys: They bought the first lots ever sold in Snoqualmie, and Edmond Kinsey built the first hotel there.

Clarke Kinsey established a photography studio in Snoqualmie in the early 1890's. During the gold rush, he and his brother Clarence operated a photography studio in Grand Forks, Yukon Territory, and also prospected for gold.

The beautiful pictures made by the Kinsey brothers of early day logging and other activities have gained nationwide recognition, and many have been reprinted in book form.

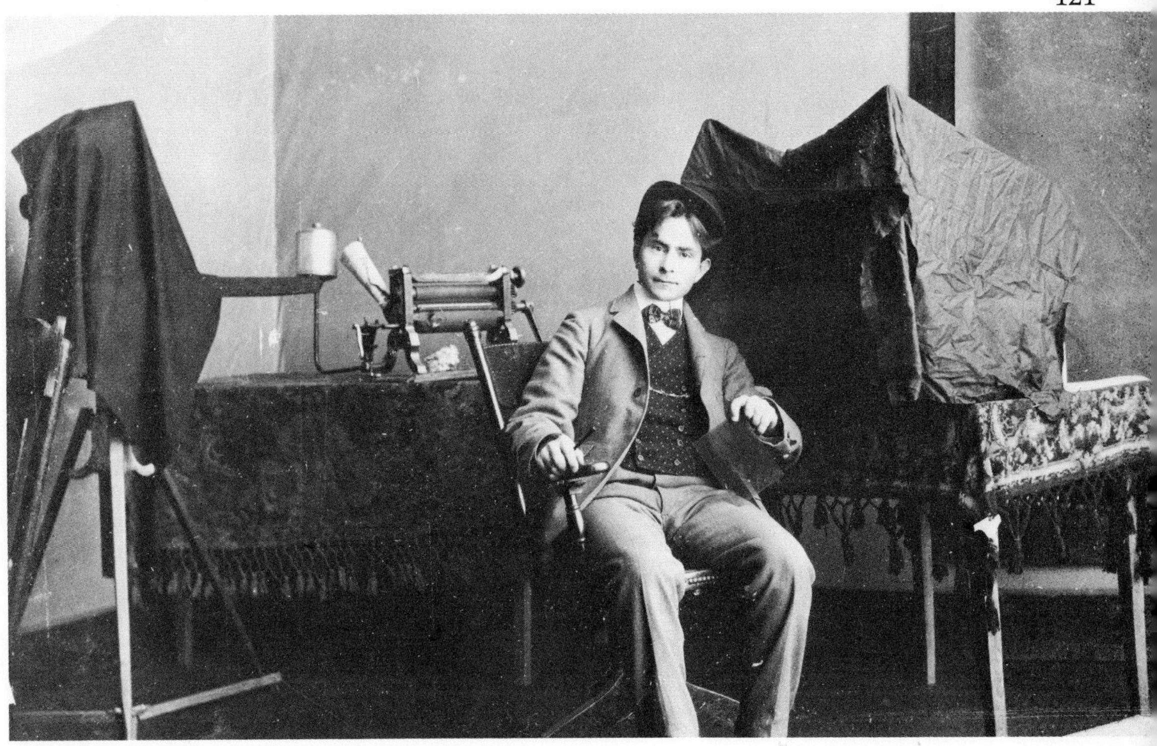

Clarke Kinsey in his studio, probably in the Klondike, although possibly at Snoqualmie.

Mr. Kinsey also became a nationally known figure through his work with West Coast Lumberman's Association. He became associated with the organization soon after his return to Seattle in 1906.

Clarke Kinsey's obituary is reprinted with permission from the Snoqualmie Valley Record, *1956. After Clarke's death, the Kinsey family donated a collection of approximately 10,000 of his eleven- by fourteen-inch timber-industry negatives to the University of Washington in Seattle.*

Leonard Kinsey, Clarke and Mary's first son, posing with one of his father's large view cameras in Grand Forks. Born in Washington in November 1900, Leonard died of diphtheria in 1907.

Acknowledgments

In one significant way, Jack Wills was more important to this book than anyone else. Jack introduced me to Ron Kinsey Jr., Clarke Kinsey's grandson. Jack spent many long hours in his darkroom turning old Kinsey glass-plate negatives into usable prints. Ron and his wife Carola shared my enthusiasm for this project and spent several evenings talking with Ron's father (Clarke's son) and Olive Kinsey Powers (Clarence's daughter), both of whom were born in Grand Forks during the gold rush era.

Numerous people were very generous with their time in helping me compile historical information for the text. These included Clayton Betts of Burnaby, British Columbia, who also loaned rare reference materials; Jim Kingsley of Parksville, British Columbia, one of the few people alive today who lived at Grand Forks; Ethel Russell Moyer of Seattle who, as a child, also lived at Grand Forks; Kathy Jones-Gates, director of the Dawson Museum and Historical Society; Carl Betke, assistant historian for the Royal Canadian Mounted Police in Ottawa; Christine Laing of Seattle, who helped with research and with several stages of the long editing process; Virginia Heiner of College, Alaska; Sarah Eppenbach of Juneau, whose research for an earlier project proved helpful in this one as well; Iris Warner of Whitehorse; several people on the staff of the Yukon Territorial Archives in Whitehorse, including Diane Johnson, William Oppen and Jennifer Heron; Sarah Levant (who did preliminary editing) and Margy Kotick, of Alaska Northwest Publishing Company; and Art Fry, who today mines the ground that was once part of Grand Forks.

Pierre Berton, perhaps the most well-known and accurate author on the Klondike, provided excellent research material in his books. He was also gracious enough to review this manuscript prior to publication and to write introductory comments to this text, for which I am very grateful.

Archie Satterfield, author of *Chilkoot Pass* and many other fine books, was also kind enough to lend his expertise.

And without one man's help this book could never have been completed: Robert N. De Armond of Alaska Northwest Publishing Company provided guidance and expert advice that simply was unavailable from anyone else.

Bibliography

Many publications provided the background information for this book, but of these dozens of books, periodicals and miscellaneous publications, a great number contained erroneous information. Many had valuable facts and information that filled gaps about what Grand

Forks life was really like, but at the same time the authors often relied on second- and third-hand information and recollections distorted by the years. Unfortunately, some of the most helpful books are often also filled with incorrect facts.

All readers, in doing any research on the Klondike, are urged to remember that perhaps as many as 90 percent of the books written on the subject contain misinformation. Periodicals of the time offer the best insight into what Klondikers did from day to day, how they worked, what they felt and why they were in the country. Many of the books written in the early part of the 20th century are some of the least credible; too many contain hearsay accounts of what happened, turned into false first-person stories of Klondike living.

Four institutions have among them an unbelievable wealth of *factual* material on the Klondike. These are the Yukon Territorial Archives at Whitehorse, the Dawson Museum & Historical Society at Dawson City, the Suzallo Library of the University of Washington in Seattle and the Alaska State Historical Library in Juneau. The material found in these places includes not only published material but public and private records as well.

A very few publications offer accurate overviews of the gold rush, and even those published during the Klondike period were very lax with their facts. Names were often misspelled and dates and facts were seldom checked for accuracy. The journalists of the day relied almost exclusively on retold stories rather than

on firsthand reporting. But there are no better sources for obtaining a *feeling* for what it was like living and working in the Klondike.

The following sources were used during research for this book; they are accompanied by notes which may be helpful for those wishing to do more reading on a particular subject.

PERSONAL RECOLLECTIONS

James E. Kingsley Sr., who lived in Grand Forks, where his father owned several businesses during a four-year period after the turn of the century.

Ronald Kinsey Sr. (son of Clarke and Mary), born in 1902 at Grand Forks.

Ethel Russell Moyer, who lived as a child in Grand Forks, where her father operated the Vendome Hotel.

Olive Kinsey Powers (daughter of Clarence and Agnes), born in 1904 at Grand Forks.

BOOKS

Adney, Tappen. *Klondike Stampede.* New York: Harper Brothers, 1900.

Berton, Pierre. *Klondike.* Toronto and New York: McLelland and Stewart, 1958. (The book was published in the United States by Alfred A. Knopf under the title *Klondike Fever.* The Canadian version has been revised, with 15,000 words of new text added.) Berton's book is the single best publication available on the Klondike. It not only reads well, but is the most factually accurate overview of the Klondike and includes a complete bibliography.

Bankson, Russel A. *The Klondike Nugget.* Caldwell, Idaho: Caxton Printers, 1935.

Bohn, David. *Kinsey, Photographer: A Half Century of Negatives of Darius and Tabitha May Kinsey.* San Francisco: Chronicle Books, 1978.

De Armond, R.N. *"Stroller" White, Tales of a Klondike Newsman.* Vancouver: Mitchell Press Ltd., 1969. De Armond, who provided expert guidance throughout the research of this book, is one of the most knowledgable individuals regarding the Klondike; any publication with which he is associated can be read with the assurance that it is factually sound.

Green, Lewis. *The Gold Hustlers.* Anchorage: Alaska Northwest Publishing Company, 1977.

Mills, Thora McIlroy. *The Church and the Klondike Gold Rush.* Toronto: United Church Publishing House, 1977.

Morgan, Murray, with photos by E.A. Hegg. *One Man's Gold Rush.* Seattle: University of Washington Press, 1967. One of the accurate books on the Klondike, with excellent photographs.

Ogilvie, William. *Early Days on the Yukon & The Story of Its Gold Finds.* The Klondike Official Guide, 1898.

Satterfield, Archie. *Chilkoot Pass, Then and Now.* Anchorage: Alaska Northwest

Publishing Company, 1973. The revised 1978 edition includes new information.

Wickersham, James. *Old Yukon: Tales, Trails and Trials.* Saint Paul, Minnesota: West Publishing, 1938. Although written by a man who was one of Alaska's foremost lawmakers, the book does contain inaccuracies.

The following books are interesting and helpful reading, but in many repsects fall into that category of questionable sources.

Armstrong, Major Nevill A.D. *Yukon Yesterdays: Thirty Years of Adventure in the Klondike.* London: John Long, Ltd., 1936.

Day, Luella. *The Tragedy of the Klondike.* New York: 1906.

Cohen, Stan. *The Streets Were Paved with Gold: A Pictorial History of the Klondike Gold Rush 1896-1899.* Missoula, Montana: Pictorial Histories Publishing Company, 1977.

Morgan, Edward E.P., with Woods, Henry. *God's Loaded Dice. Alaska 1897-1930.* Caldwell, Idaho: Caxton Printers, 1948.

Palmer, Frederick. *In the Klondyke, Including an Account of a Winter's Journey to Dawson.* New York: Charles Scribner's Sons, 1899.

PAMPHLETS AND BROCHURES

Northern Navigation Company. *To the Alaska Gold Fields.* San Francisco: 1907.

Report of the Commissioner of Mines, Territory of Alaska. Juneau: 1938.

Schrader, F.C. and Spencer, A.C. *The Geology and Mineral Resources of a Portion of the*

Copper River District, Alaska. Department of the Interior, U.S. Geological Survey, 1901.

Stanton, James B. *Ho For the Klondike: A Whimsical Look at the Years 1897-1898.* Vancouver, British Columbia: Centennial Museum, 1970.

Wold, Jo Anne. *Fairbanks: The $200 Million Gold Rush Town.* Fairbanks: 1971.

The Yukon Illustrated. (a ten-part publication). Dawson: 1905.

Zaccarelli's Book Store. Dawson: 1908.

PERIODICALS

ALASKA® magazine and *The ALASKA JOURNAL®*, numerous articles from 1935 to the present. The articles are indexed and available from Alaska Northwest Publishing Company, Box 4-EEE, Anchorage, Alaska 99509.

Alaska Mining Record, numerous editions. Juneau: 1897.

Alaska Searchlight, A Literary and News Journal of the North, numerous editions. Juneau: 1897.

Dawson Daily News, Summer Mining Edition, 1899, and all editions from January 9, 1900, to May 31, 1904, and the Klondike Special, August 16, 1913, and various other editions.

Fairbanks Times, various editions. 1911.

Klondike Nugget, 1898-1899 and 1902-1903.

MacKay, Wallace Vincent. "Belinda." *Seattle Times, Charmed Land Magazine.* August 12, 1962.

"Parksville's Jim Kingsley." *Daily Colonist,* Victoria: February 29, 1976.

"She Was the Richest Woman in the Klondike." *Weekend Magazine,* Volume 12 (1962) Montreal.

Snoqualmie Valley Record, December 6, 1956.

White Horse Tribune, Summer, 1975. Special issue.

Shorey's Bookstore in Seattle has one of the most extensive collections of Alaskana and books on the North for sale anywhere, and the store also reprints dozens of publications in limited editions, including:

Cadell, H.M. "The Klondike and Yukon Goldfield in 1913." *Smithsonian Report, 1914.* Reprinted from *The Scottish Geographical Magazine,* July 1914.

Curtis, Edward S. " The Rush to the Klondike Over the Mountain Passes." *Century Magazine,* March 1898.

Klondike News Volume I, Number I. (April 1, 1898). Interesting but with numerous factual errors.

London, Jack. "The Gold-Hunters of the North." *Atlantic Monthly Magazine,* July 1903.

Webb, John Sidney. "The River Trip to the Klondike." *Century Magazine,* March 1898.

MISCELLANEOUS

The four institutions cited earlier have on file volumes and volumes of unpublished private and public records. Those records used for research on this project included correspondence between private parties and government officials, and between government

employees and government officials in the Yukon, Dawson and Grand Forks. Among those records used were documents and the correspondence of the Yukon Territorial Commissioner, the Yukon Board of Education, the North West Mounted Police (Yukon Territory; B Detachment, Dawson; and Bonanza Detachment, Grand Forks), Crown Timber and Land agents, Dawson, and the Canadian Department of the Interior.

Also, *Alaska Mining History: A Source Document,* written and compiled by Virginia Doyle Heiner, was issued in 1977. The bibliography, although dealing mostly with Alaska, also contains information on a great many publications covering the Klondike. It was published by the University of Alaska Museum, Anchorage.

When gold was discovered in Nome in 1899, Clarke and Clarence Kinsey decided to try their luck there. They repainted their sled, adding the word Nome *in large letters, and headed west. However, just as Dawson was not to their liking when they first arrived in the north, Nome also was too hectic. So the Kinseys stayed only briefly and then headed back to Grand Forks, their permanent home. They mined, they photographed and they built lives for themselves as part of that growing community. They stayed long enough to watch Grand Forks grow and thrive, stabilize and settle into the 20th century—then shrink and fade as the gold began to disappear.*